FLY FISHING
THE LAKES

FLY FISHING THE LAKES

Rex Gerlach

WINCHESTER PRESS

Book & Jacket Design by George H. Buehler

Library of Congress Catalog Card Number: 72-79358
ISBN: 0-87691-075-4

Published by Winchester Press
460 Park Avenue, New York   10022

Printed in the United States of America

To my dad, Ray Gerlach,
who first awakened in me
a love of the lakes, streams and forests,
and all the wonderful
creatures that dwell therein.

Acknowledgments

First, I want to give special thanks to my regular fly fishing companions of the past 20 years, Fenton Roskelley, outdoor editor of the Spokane *Daily Chronicle;* and Thomas H. Stouffer, U.S.A.F. (ret.), for their invaluable contributions of time, patience and effort in developing and researching many of the techniques described in this book.

My most sincere gratitude also goes to veteran Washington State Game Dept. fisheries biologist Don E. Earnest, who helped me convert the technical aspects of limnology into understandable lay language.

I am also deeply indebted to many Canadian government officials and anglers, without whose valued assistance the sections on arctic grayling and northern pike would have been lacking in scope. They include: Roland Boire, Deputy Director, Canadian Government Travel Bureau, Ottawa; Thomas L. Hill, Canadian Government Travel Bureau, Seattle; Hon. G. L. Colborne, P. Eng.; C. S. "Toar" Springstein, Director, Tourist Branch, Saskatchewan Dept. of Industry; Alan Hill, a consultant with that same Branch; George E.

Couldwell, Director of Fisheries, Saskatchewan Dept. of Natural Resources; Jim and Ted Jackson of Waterbury Lake Lodge, Sask.; James H. Thurston of Snowbird Lake Lodge, N. W. T.; Doug Hill and Mel Jamieson of Wollaston Lake Lodge, Sask.; the late Miss Evelyn Miller; John Guldner; Harvey Dryden; Stuart Smith; R. J. Paterson; Frank Bishop; R. R. Andrews; Myles Crowley; Arthur Higgs; John Whittaker; Jack Lambert; and Lionel Hachey.

I also want to thank the following expert anglers for their invaluable technical advice aimed at making this book a truly helpful study of lake fly fishing fundamentals: Dan Bailey; Gordon Baker; Bill Cairns; Hon. Claude Batault; Prof. Henry Bugbee, Ph.D.; Dave Carlson; Everett Caryl, Sr.; Dr. A. A. Cunningham, D.D.S.; Bob Elliott; Jim Green; Mike Kennedy; Dale LeFollette; Fred Locke; Ray MacPherson; Bud Lilly; Leonard Miracle; Donald L. Manahan; Joe D. Miotke; Gil Nyerges; E. H. "Polly" Rosborough; Ben Silknitter; Rod Towsley; Ted Trueblood; Milt Kahl; Tim Vaughn; Bob Wethern; and the late Frank Wire. Further thanks go to Fenton Roskelley for the photographs on pages 43 and 62, and to Al Cunningham for those on pages 19 and 60.

To these and all the rest of my fly fishing friends and acquaintances who have contributed their thoughts and the benefit of their experience to this book goes my deepest gratitude.

Contents

Introduction

It seems ironic that fly fishing shows signs of maturing as a sport in America, that technology has provided anglers with superbly efficient fly fishing tools at prices with mass appeal precisely at a time when, at least in the U.S.A., the future of our moving waters seems in jeopardy.

Pollution, dying watersheds, dams and increasing numbers of anglers are steadily encroaching on the productivity and pleasure of stream fishing in the United States. The whittling away of our nation's stream and river resources—often under the insidious guise of socio-economic development—appears to be taking on an irreversible trend. Much of this so-called "progress" involving our moving waters results in angling pressures far in excess of many streams' fish-producing capabilities.

Future stream fishing prospects within the U.S. borders probably wouldn't be bright even if the present economic water "war" didn't steam up the overall picture.

It's been estimated that the number of sport fishermen in the nation will more than double by the year A.D. 2000. With no pro-portionate increase in the number of miles of fishable free-flowing waterways in sight, about all fly fishermen of the present era can look forward to is additional competition from other anglers for casting room. Already, the number of anglers using our public streams is so great it's difficult at times to make a back-cast for fear of hooking another recreation-hungry lad or lassie in the seat of the waders.

Where then will fly fishermen find relatively uncrowded waters in the foreseeable future? Certainly, the remotest regions of Alaska and Canada will attract more attention from angling enthusiasts seeking solitude. No doubt there will also be a tremendous increase in fly fishing for saltwater game fish along the Atlantic, Gulf Coast and Pacific seaboard states.

For the most part, however, inland anglers will be forced to con-centrate most of their efforts on the ponds, lakes, reservoirs and impoundments that dot the national landscape. American sport fish-ermen eventually will be "forced" to fish in lakes, because by far the most significant increase in future sport fish habitat will come about as a direct result of the construction of additional man-made lakes.

One authoritative study predicts that by A.D. 2000 the catch of game fish per surface acre of water *must* increase by 65 percent over that now made on existing waters in order to keep up with the demand of the 60-odd-million anglers who will be flocking to fishable waters. The study concludes that only man-made lakes will be cap-able of taking up the angling overload, lakes being usually more manageable and productive per surface acre than most streams.

Angler interest is already shifting from streams to lakes in some regions. Fishing opportunities have been greatly enhanced, both quantitatively and qualitatively, through intelligently conceived lake management programs in several important U.S. lake regions.

Although most state fish management people now do their best to provide adequate public fishing opportunities, their future efforts appear to be an uphill battle. Not only will it become increasingly difficult for state fish and game departments to maintain both the quantity and the quality of angling we fishermen have come to expect, but there will be considerable resistance from many of us faced with the realities of transition from stream to lake fishing!

The modern revolution in lake fly fishing methods described

throughout the following chapters was brought about, at least in part, by the introduction in 1948 of sinking fly lines (Fig. 43)—lines designed specifically to carry flies deeply and rapidly down to the fish. Sinking fly lines are the answer to the prayers of generations of frustrated lake fishermen. Before their introduction, anglers dosed their old-style silk fly lines with numerous relatively ineffective and sometimes offensive preparations, in order to promote their sinking.

I shudder to recall how I used to rub the finish of an expensive silk fly line with anything from toothpaste to powdered graphite! These lines sank all right, but never as fast as I wanted them to. To top it off, the graphite treatment ruined the beautiful oiled line finish and constantly kept my fingers smeared a dirty gray black color.

The new sinking lines are smooth-casting, long-lasting lines that take your flies down quickly to where the fish are. Together with today's superior floating lines and a number of special-purpose lines, like those with sinking tip sections, effective fly fishing of the lakes is not only possible, but a decided pleasure!

Amazing progress has been made along the lines of popularizing the sport of fly fishing by dedicated enthusiasts like the Federation of Fly Fishermen. Dozens of new regional and local fly fishing clubs and associations have formed throughout the country in the past few years. The almost religious zeal of modern-day fly fishing "missionaries" has been contagious. Fly fishermen, as a group, are actively organizing and spreading their "gospel" to hundreds of eager-to-learn postulants each year. Simultaneously, tackle shops, guest ranches and fishing tackle manufacturers are providing specialized fly fishing schools designed specifically to educate the novices. Sportsmens' associations and fly fishing clubs conduct fly fishing clinics throughout the country for the same purpose. Why? The answer is simple. Modern fly fishermen in America are, for the most part, anxious for other anglers to share in the fun. Fly fishing is superb fun! And, when a man fly fishes entire new worlds of angling enjoyment are open to him.

If you were raised in the great tradition of worm-threading, salmon egg-soaking, water-dogging, plug-casting, and juggin' for cats— as many of us were—you probably fished blithely along under the false assumption that you were getting the most out of the sport. But fishermen, like golfers, go through many phases of development. Chances are that one day out on the lake you were complacently enveloped in that euphoric state of mind commonly known as "worm-threaderosis." Your rod tip was trembling nervously while a big old bass massaged your night-crawler's hide with his lips. You had a hefty stringer of good-sized largemouths hanging over the side—testimony to the angling world of your unquestionable proficiency. That night you slept the sleep of the innocent. And, the next day at the barbershop you might have even done a little bragging—with that smug humility possessed only by a true fisherman.

A couple of days passed. Then you went fishing again; same spot, same bait. But, this time the fish weren't biting—or so you concluded until just before dark when a strange apparition appeared on the water. It was a medium-sized, manlike creature, standing up in its boat and waving a long flexible pole to which appeared to be affixed a small ship's hawser. The creature appeared to be fishing with something resembling a dead mouse or bat.

You shook your head in sympathy for the misdirected and obviously demented creature. Suddenly, however, moments after the "dead mouse" had landed on the water there was a tremendous splash and a great, bronze-backed lunker bass erupted out of the lily pads, firmly affixed to that strange creature's line. Minutes later the six-pounder was lifted from the water by the lower lip. Being generous as you are, you probably muttered something like "pretty lucky" under your breath and went back to threading on a new worm. But, when the creature landed two more big bass in short order and broke off on a bigger one, you couldn't take the strain. You probably sneaked quietly away towards home dragging your ego behind you. It happened that way to me; I know!

By the next time you went fishing you had sufficiently recovered from that first traumatic evening to row over to the strange creature and inquire "Whatchafishinwith?" "Deerhairmouse" was the startling reply. "Canisee't?" you asked with fuming disbelief. And, can you recall your unabashed amazement when that strange creature, who called himself a fly fisherman, put on another display of the attractiveness of that now quite bedraggled deer-hair mouse?

"Maybe there is something to all this fly fishin' baloney after all!" you probably concluded with grim resignation. "But, I'll be damned if I'll get all hung up in all that expensive and silly looking paraphernalia, bugs, flies, light leaders, bamboo rods 'n all that stuff! Not me! I'm a real fisherman, not a tackle tinkerer."

On the other hand, you might have reacted to the lesson like rapidly increasing numbers of American anglers. You might have reasoned that maybe, just maybe, there were times when fly fishing was the most productive way to fish.

If you did . . . hallelujah Brother! You've been saved! Because fly fishing is in fact at times the most effective way to catch many of the most popular freshwater game fish species. And you, friend, are on the way to becoming a complete angler in every sense of the word. What you will soon learn is that fly fishing isn't as difficult as you might think. Nor is it a sport financially beyond the means of men with modest incomes. Fly fishing is a fun game for everyone, a wonderfully compatible companion sport for anglers who excell at bait-fishing, plug-casting, rubber-worming, spinning and juggin' for cats. There's a time and place for all of these delightful aspects of fishing. Fly fishing is one of the most exciting.

Fly fishing has been considered by its most avid devotees the most contemplative form of angling for centuries. Non fly-fishermen tend to interpret the contemplative aspects of the sport to be overly academic, pseudo-poetic pie-in-the-sky. Nothing could be further from the truth. At a meeting of the Federation of Fly Fishermen I once heard famed Lee Wulff say that "fly fishing is all things to all people." He was absolutely correct. One can be either as pragmatic and objective as a scientist or as aesthetically motivated as Michelangelo in both his approach to and practice of fly fishing. And thankfully, he can catch fish with either attitude! Consistent success via either approach requires concentration, however.

Concentrating one's full attention on a vast assortment of sometimes apparently unrelated details like water temperatures, feeding patterns, insect activity, casting technique, subtle nuances of retrieve, leader tippet size, and small boat handling isn't easy for some people to accomplish. However, it can vastly improve one's numerical catch of fish. I can't tell you how much concentration to inject into your own fishing. That's for you to decide. Some men need to focus their attention intently on a sport to derive pleasure and benefit from it. Others seem to require semidetachment from the world around them. Because many anglers fly fish for recreation—not for fish in the pot —it is unfair to sit in judgment on either attitude. But the fact remains that intense concentration produces more fish in the bag than daydreaming. Keep an angling log for several years, recording not only the weather, catch and other physical data of each trip, but also your own mental attitudes. You'll be surprised what your notes will tell you later about *you* as a fisherman! This leads to what is possibly the most important human factor influencing one's effectiveness as a fly fisherman . . . the willingness to *experiment!*

Thoughtful, knowledgeable, imaginative selection of angling areas and fly patterns; the rate, depth and angle of retrieve; and the method by which one approaches feeding game fish is the cement between fishing theory and fishing practice. Some excellent fly fishermen experiment instinctively with a kind of uncanny intuition. They're the fellows normally referred to as "born fishermen," because they seem to know precisely what fly to use, where to fish it and what retrieve to employ. Fortunately for the fish, the rest of us must develop an ability to succeed with a fly rod through a constant, never-ending process of study and practice, trial and error.

A good example of the worth of experimentation took place on a favorite brook trout pond. During the early morning hours two of us hooked and released a dozen chunky brookies on size 6 Colonel Bates streamer flies. Then, about nine o'clock the fish stopped biting, or so it seemed. We began to try other types of wet flies, including shrimp patterns, nymphs and leechlike streamers. For an hour or more our frustration mounted as we changed flies, lengthened leaders and experimented fruitlessly with variations in retrieve.

Then my companion noted the presence of fair numbers of hatched midges on the surface film. He tied a size 14 fly suggesting a midge pupa to his tippet and began to work it slowly along the lake bottom using a "hand-twist" retrieve, which we'll discuss later in detail. On his second cast with the small nymph a three-pound brook trout grabbed the fly as it started to rise to the surface, like a natural pupa rising to hatch. He killed the fish and checked the contents of its stomach. The trout's gullet was crammed with midge pupae and larvae. We concluded and verified by his catching a dozen trout on the tiny nymph that the brookies had not quit feeding at nine o'clock when they stopped taking our streamers. The fish had merely "shifted gears" and begun to feed on the abundant midges. Unfortunately, I missed out on some of the fun that day as a result of being bull-headed and determined to catch all my fish on streamer flies. My stubborn refusal to accept the facts before my eyes cost me a share in the fun.

In its most effective forms, experimentation during a fishing situation consists of methodically exploring all the various possible combinations of locating the game fish and interesting them in artificials. Under most conditions water temperature will provide the tip-off as to where the fish are. Observation of aquatic insect activity, or the lack of it, usually yields additional clues as to what flies to use and where to fish them.

For example, if the temperature of the lake is less than 40 degrees at the surface, chances are the fish will be relatively inactive and respond most readily to slowly fished streamers 'and nymphs, fished on sinking fly lines near the lake bottom. On the other hand, if the water temperature lies between 50 and 65 degrees at the surface, strong possibilities exist for insect hatches and consequent surface and near-surface feeding. Under optimum water temperatures, expect action at any of several depths during a day of fly fishing and be prepared accordingly to fish in surface waters as well as near the lake bottom. The knowledge gained from a season or two of fishing a particular lake might suggest which fly patterns and which areas of the lake offer the best chances of producing action during a particular season of the year. In this way experimentation is anything but a haphazard affair. The more you learn about each specific lake, its fish and other aquatic creatures, the more generally effective your fishing of that lake becomes. Each lake is similar to, but in many ways different from all others. It's almost always more difficult to catch fish consistently in unfamiliar waters than in lakes one knows as intimately as his back yard. Each lake, like each trout stream, must be learned by a process of observation and experimentation. Fly fishing is not a sport at which anyone becomes an instant expert. That takes years to accomplish. The more one fishes, the more firmly convinced he usually becomes there are no expert fishermen, only better fishermen by varying degrees—and luckier fishermen!

Experience in fishing various types of lakes for different species of game fish eventually teaches that "timing" is one of the most important pages in the fly fisher's book of so-called tricks. Knowing what we do about the seasonality of aquatic insect hatches and the effects of water temperature upon the behavior of fish and their food organisms, it would be utterly ridiculous to ignore the matter of proper timing in planning lake fishing.

Accurate logs of fishing experiences can be most helpful in the planning of fishing escapades for the coming year. It is very useful to have a record of the names of the lakes and streams one fishes, the weather conditions, movements of forage fish, predominant insect hatches each season, effective fly patterns, and extraneous experiences that occurred while fishing there. In the case of remote, seldom revisited waters, notes regarding the route traveled are often invaluable. The few moments it takes to record the essential data about a lake are time well invested in future angling pleasure and success.

This sort of general angling schedule takes little effort to prepare, and coupled with a solid, working knowledge of lake ecology gives enough direction to one's fishing to keep a fellow more or less on the track in his never-ending search for the excitement provided by a pulsating rod tip. The amount of detail you personally incorporate into a plan for fishing the waters of your home region will depend entirely on you and whether you have time to merely sample the fishing or a desire to wet a line in every lake within two hundred miles of your doorstep. The important thing is to properly time fishing to those waters presenting the best seasonal opportunities.

It's the purpose of this book to awaken both neophyte and veteran fishing devotees to the incredible variety of exciting angling opportunities awaiting them on lakes, and to provide a solid base of knowledge about lakes and their inhabitants to assist the "new" lake fisherman in capitalizing on the still-water fly fishing bonanza.

Chapter I is essential to understanding the remainder of the text in that it contains much of the fundamental knowledge about aquatic creatures and lakes that influences angling techniques described in later chapters.

Please note that the chapters on tackle and casting deal mostly with *essential* techniques and pieces of equipment. A long discussion of tackle, while it might possibly be interesting and informative, would tend to draw attention away from the all-important "fishing" aspects. The same thing holds true for the chapter on casting. Numerous fine casting texts and booklets are already available. This book makes no attempt to compete with them except where techniques essential to effective lake fishing are involved.

FLY FISHING
THE LAKES

1

The Lake Environment and How To Approach It

It's usually a lot harder to find fish in lakes than it is to catch them. The physical characteristics and relationships of aquatic animals and plants to their environment and to one another contribute to the problem, because lakes are rather like people . . . both similar to, and different from, in varying degrees, all the rest.

In some ways, lakes can be compared to large, popular restaurants catering to cosmopolitan communities like New York and San Francisco, where the diners' tastes and appetites may vary seasonally and ethnically.

Nature's bill of fare for lake game fish is strongly influenced by seasonal cycles in the aquatic climate that change the availability and activity of the fish food organisms themselves.

Taking a closer look at lakes, fly fishermen see them as highly complex bodies of water surrounded by land. Some lakes are as fertile as the richest truck-gardens. The bottoms of these rich lakes are carpeted to varying extents with aquatic plants that encourage

1

production of basic fish food organisms like aquatic insect nymphs, mollusks and crustaceans.

Certain other kinds of lakes contain so little aquatic vegetation and natural fish food that they can't support significant populations of game fish. Biologists usually refer to them as "sterile," since their fish food production capabilities are virtually nil.

As fly fishermen we're only interested in lakes containing significant amounts of aquatic life. Both the physical characteristics of lakes and the types of fish foods found in productive lakes influence our angling methods.

There are two main types of productive freshwater lakes. Those which have no inlets or outlets, which are totally landlocked and receive all their water from springs, run-off and rain are called "seepage" lakes. The other main type of freshwater lake is one which has inlets or outlets, or both. It's called a "drainage" or "flowage" lake, and for our purposes can be grouped with man-made reservoirs and impoundments of streams and rivers. We differentiate between these two main lake types because of the different angling methods sometimes necessary to fish them effectively.

Lakes have other significant physical traits that help determine how to fish them with flies—or, for that matter, with any sort of natural bait or artificial lure. Actually, the factors discussed in this chapter will be helpful to virtually any lake fisherman, regardless of his preferred angling method.

Lakes can also be classified as "deep" or "shallow"; "clear" or "turbid"; "alkaline," "neutral," or "soft-watered"; all of which conditions can exist alone or together in an almost infinite combination.

Let's consider all of these factors and see how they affect fishing.

The depth of a lake strongly influences fly fishing methods. Let's look at some common types of deep lakes first, because they're usually the most difficult in which to locate fish.

From a fly fisherman's viewpoint, deep lakes are those in which a preponderance of the water volume exists at depths in excess of 25 feet.

Interrelated with water depth is the temperature of the water, which also strongly influences angling methods. The location of fish at any given moment, their disposition towards feeding and the activities of fish food organisms all relate intimately to water temperature.

Lakes Form into Layers

Few anglers, even among the most experienced, really understand why every level of most deep lakes cannot support fish life throughout the entire year. The primary reason is that most deep lakes divide into several sharply defined layers or "strata" during the summer months. From the surface down, a typical deep lake is divided into well defined temperature-oxygen layers called the surface film, or "meniscus"; the top layer or "epilimnion"; a middle layer termed the "thermocline" or "mesolimnion"; and a bottom layer of water called the "hypolimnion" (Fig. 1).

The scientists' names for the various water layers are included here only so you'll be able to understand the jargon if you decide to study texts on the subject of limnology. Throughout the remainder of this book water layers will be referred to by their lay names.

Finding lake fishes during the summer months would be a cinch if the various strata of water were always at the same levels in all deep lakes. But, they aren't!

The top layer of water in a typical deep lake may extend down from the surface eight or more feet during late spring (Fig. 2). Yet, by the time the first leaves color up in early fall, that identical top layer may conceivably plunge down over 50 feet in some very clear

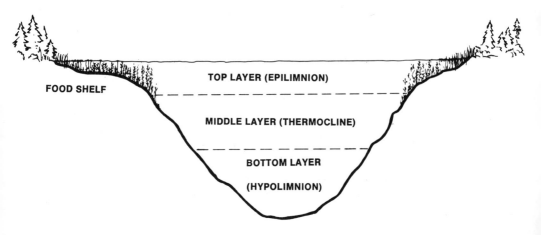

Fig. 1. *Layers of a deep lake.*

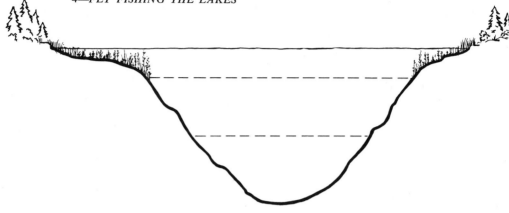

Fig. 2.   *Layers of a deep lake in the late spring.*

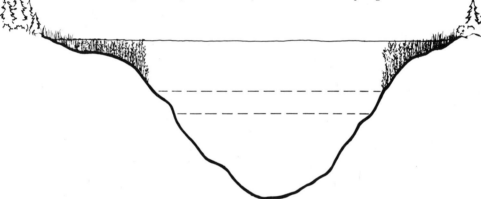

Fig. 3.   *Layers of a deep lake during the summer stagnation period.*

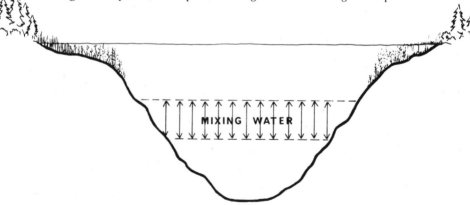

MIXING WATER

Fig. 4.   *Layers of a deep lake in the fall overturn.*

lakes, although the average would probably be in the neighborhood of 20 feet in a temperate zone lake of normal clarity (Fig. 3).

Fortunately for the fish, that top layer is usually well supplied with oxygen in all deep lakes in the summer. The amount of oxygen in the lower layers of water in deep lakes during the summer depends on how much organic material decomposes in the water after it begins to form layers in the spring.

The middle and bottom water layers in deep, stratified lakes in the summer are always colder than the top layer. However, as attractive as cool depths are to certain gamefish species when the top layer is warm, most fish will tend to avoid great depths because they frequently contain insufficient oxygen to sustain life.

Temperature isn't the only regulator of fish behavior in the summer. Most freshwater game fish are well endowed by Nature to withstand the norms of extreme temperature they encounter both in summer and winter. Most of the lake game fishes can tolerate water temperatures well into the 70s. They may not like it, but they can live in it, at least for brief periods of time.

What causes the waters of most deep lakes to divide into temperature-oxygen layers? In some ways water reacts to cooling and warming like the air we breathe.

School-age tots learn that warm air rises and cool air descends. Cooling and warming waters also fall and rise. As the tamaracks flick their saffron lashes across Earth's green cheeks, frosty nights and chilly days cool the top layers of the lakes. The cool water sinks (Fig. 4). Eventually, the cooling top layer sinks right through the middle and bottom layers of deep lakes and a complete mixing of the waters takes place. This mixing usually occurs over a relatively long period of time, in temperate zones usually more than a month.

Once all three layers of water are completely mixed the oxygen content is uniform throughout the lake. The water temperature reaches a point of equality from top to bottom, 39.2° F.

This phenomenon is commonly called the fall "overturn" of a lake. It's Nature's way of replenishing the oxygen supply in lake water through wave action and the sinking of cool waters. The lake remains in this turned-over condition for about a month.

Overturn has a dramatic effect on the behavior of fish. In a sense, it resembles unleashing a genie from a bottle. Throughout the entire summer all the fish in the deep lake are restricted by their need for oxygen into a single, relatively narrow belt of water extending down-wards from the surface. Then the lake turns over, mixing enough oxygen into all parts of the lake to sustain aquatic life. Naturally, the fish soon discover they can safely swim into virtually every nook and cranny of the lake. As a result, during these overturn periods the fish tend to disperse in varying degrees throughout deep lakes, all of which can make for very uncertain angling opportunities.

During the winter months, especially if the lake is covered by ice, the oxygen supply in the water again suffers depletion from organic decomposition and aquatic animal respiration (Fig. 5).

Nature once again injects a fresh oxygen supply into the lake during the following spring. The ice goes out. When the ice breaks up, the surface water temperature is 32° F. The surface of the lake begins to warm under the influence of higher air temperature and wave action. Oxygen is quickly whipped into the surface waters by the waves.

Because the maximum density of water is slightly below 40° F., either colder or warmer waters will float. At ice-out time, as the surface waters warm above 32° F, colder waters immediately below them come to the surface. Slightly warmed waters sink, pushing previously warmed waters deeper. The cold water at the bottom of the lake rises and is warmed. Usually, within 24 hours of ice-out, the temperature of the water throughout a deep lake reaches a uni-

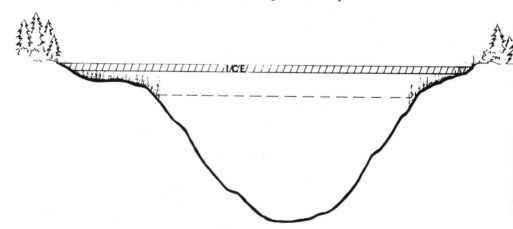

Fig. 5. *Layers of a deep lake during the winter stagnation period.*

form 39.2° F. Once again the oxygen content of the lake from top to bottom becomes uniform and the spring overturn of the lake is completed.

Stratification and summer stagnation then begin. Breezes whip oxygen from the air into the waters at the surface. As the oxygenating process continues, the warming surface waters begin to float on the cooler waters below rather like heavy cream on a liqueur. Normally, Nature virtually seals off the bottoms of deep lakes from the upper layers of water by June in most temperate zones.

Since fish require both oxygen and food for survival it's now relatively easy to conclude where they are to be found during the various seasons of the year: relatively scattered following the spring and fall overturn periods, increasingly restricted to middle and surface layers during winter and summer stagnation.

Other factors assist in pinning down the probable locations of lake game fish. For example, some species show exceptional tolerances for water over 70° F. They're usually referred to as "warmwater" fishes and include the perches, crappies, sunfishes and largemouth bass. Most of the chars and trouts, on the other hand, accommodate best to relatively cool waters. That's why biologists generally refer to them as "cold-water" species.

It's only natural for fish with low tolerances for warm water to be drawn towards the coolest parts of deep lakes in the summer. But, that tendency doesn't mean the cold-water species won't occasionally swim into warm surface waters to feed. It's not at all uncommon to observe cold-water fishes surface feeding after sunset, even when the temperature in the top layer approaches 80° F.

Some Notable Exceptions

What we've discovered thus far about how typical deep lakes stratify is fairly true about a majority of such waters. But, there are some notable exceptions. Some very clear, deep lakes do not divide into the various temperature-oxygen layers during the summer in the usual fashion. Some deep lakes support fish populations at depths exceeding 100 feet, not at all uncommon, say, in certain gin-clear trout lakes in the Canadian Pre-Cambrian Shield and in parts of the northern U.S.A.

Shallow Lakes

Shallow lakes are easier to fly fish than deep lakes. Many shallow lakes and ponds never really stratify in the summer. They can support fish and other aquatic life forms at any depth.

From the standpoint of the fly fisherman, a shallow lake is one in which the preponderance of the water volume is 25 feet or less. This is the depth that approaches the extreme limits of our ability to fish flies by casting and retrieving methods on conventional fly fishing tackle.

Although we've characterized all lakes as either deep or shallow, the subtle differences between lakes falling into either category are astounding. For example, there are those very deep lakes just mentioned that do not stratify in the usual manner. One very common type of shallow lake or pond stratifies sharply at a depth of ten feet or thereabouts. Then, there's the kind of shallow lake that would stratify under normal conditions, but which has been rigged by fish management people with a mechanical aeration unit that injects additional air into the water to prevent stratification. And then there are lakes that exhibit no sharply defined characteristics to assist us in making positive conclusions about how, when and where to fish them.

Shallow lakes display a number of attributes that recommend them to angling by fly fishing methods. The main reason many shallow lakes favor fly fishermen is that they can be effectively probed from the surface film right down to the weeds at the bottom.

Some of the most productive shallow sport fishing lakes contain weedy areas. It's a scientific fact that certain types of aquatic plants promote the production of fish food organisms. As a result, the presence of weeds in a lake can be one of the several important, visible indicators of the probable location of game fish.

There are types of shallow lakes that supercharge a fly fisher's soul. One favorite type of lake is called a "stump ranch." Generally speaking, a stump ranch lake consists of a flowage impoundment formed by a low dam across a stream. The stump ranch lake derives its name from the underwater regions bordering the now flooded creek channel, which are usually lined with a nightmarish tangle of cut off trees, submerged brush and willows.

The resulting body of water probably varies from five to several hundred acres in area, running in depth from two to possibly 20 feet. Such a lake is frequently located in a relatively secluded valley in a cattle-raising region where the bottomland along the old stream bed was used as a pasture by several generations of landowners.

Fertilization of the valley's topsoil enriched it to a highly productive level. Once the small dam was constructed and the bottomland flooded, the ex-pasture soon became the watery Shangri-la for a multitude of aquatic plants and animals.

Within a short time, probably less than a year, certain forms of aquatic plants took root and promoted the production of untold millions of plankton, aquatic insects and crustaceans.

The sudden impact of the new superabundance of food on the game fish population in that part of the creek was dramatic in its effect.

Before the lake was formed the main fish species in the stream was probably brook trout. Chances are good that the largest brookie in the stream didn't exceed 12 inches in the days before the lake came about. When the new lake was formed, those relatively small brook trout began to shovel in the hosts of nymphs, shrimps and snails like a pride of lions gorging on a kill. Before the year ended the brook trout in the new stump ranch lake averaged a strong 10 inches in length, with numerous fish approaching 12 inches.

By the end of the second year the lake produced brookies up to 16 inches. And, when the lake was four years old, it had become quietly famous as "that place where they're catching 'em up to five pounds!"

Any fly fisherman lucky enough to discover the spot enjoyed a quality of fishing in some ways rivaling fly fishing virgin waters in distant lands.

Another type of shallow lake frequently of interest to pragmatic practitioners of piscatorial prognostication is the seepage lake or pond fed by spring water. When such a lake exists in combination with mildly alkaline water conditions, chara weed beds and a supply of freshwater shrimps, water-fleas and aquatic insects, you have the makings of a veritable "fish factory." Lakes of this type usually vary in size from a few to several hundred acres.

Flowage lakes of relatively large dimensions, natural or man-made, and having extensive shallow areas two to 20 feet deep, also are prime fly fishing possibilities. World-famous Henry's Lake in Idaho is precisely that sort of natural drainage basin. The 2,500-acre lake yields great numbers of outsized rainbow, cutthroat and brook trout to fly fishermen who probe the numerous channels between weed beds and brush piles at the inlet streams with nymph flies fished on sinking fly lines.

Large impoundments and reservoirs containing extensive shallows and an abundance of forage fish often provide fair to good fly fishing. It's true that the largest of these man-made lakes are sometimes difficult waters to "read." But, once you find the areas harboring game fish, the fly fishing rewards can be bountiful.

Other Important Factors

Turbidity of the water is another key factor affecting the where, how and what-with of lake fishing with artificial flies. Water is said to be turbid when silt, refuse or minute animal organisms become suspended in it. The most obvious effect of turbidity is a reduction in the amount of sunlight filtering down into the depths. As a result, pondweeds can't usually thrive in turbid lakes at the same extremes of depth they can in clear bodies of water. This in turn affects the fish, since they are intimately bound to aquatic animals and forage fish whose food organisms are frequently dependent on some sort of plant growth. Biologists call this interdependency between aquatic plants and animals a "food chain" (Fig. 6). Generally speaking, the plants, animals and fish in turbid lakes are found at shallower maximum depths than they are in clear lakes.

Pondweeds are another visible indicator of where to find game fish in lakes. Fisheries biologists tell us lakes with good light penetration afford the best potential for raising gamefish foods in quantity. Sunlight filtering down to the lake bottom promotes weed growth and the subsequent production of certain aquatic animals, insects and forage fish. However, it should be understood that the quantity of weed growth you observe in a lake doesn't necessarily insure that the lake will provide good fly fishing opportunities. Exceptionally dense masses of aquatic plants, for example, actually can suppress the growth and development of fish food organisms.

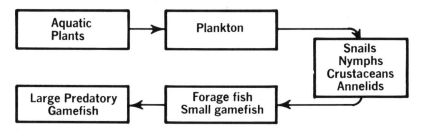

Fig. 6. *Highly simplified anatomy of the aquatic food chain.*

The quality and kinds of aquatic plants in lakes, rather than the bulk quantity of weeds, is the real tip off to that lake's fish growing capabilities.

For example, certain species of aquatic plants, like chara, tend to thrive in relatively alkaline water and promote the production of numerous fish food organisms. To catalog and illustrate all of the predominant water plants that serve in this capacity would be of little value to the average angler. It suffices to know that an abundance of sturdy, wide-leafed pondweeds in a lake (not including the lily pads) is a fairly good indicator of alkaline water where chances are excellent natural fish foods will abound.

On the other hand, a lake with only stunted, skimpy-leafed plants probably contains either neutral or soft water where food organisms are less abundant.

In rich, relatively alkaline waters containing a superabundance of fish food organisms the game fish tend to feed heavily and sporadically on some specific underwater creature like the freshwater scud (commonly called a "shrimp"), dragonfly and damselfly nymphs or snails. This fact goes without question. Long ago fly fishermen named this phenomenon "selectivity." However, what about those occasions when the fish merely seem to be feeding in a selective fashion, while in fact their gullets are crammed with several types of foods?

Actually, the hard realities of aquatic ecology put the lie to parts of the selectivity theory. Competition for, or the lack of available food, appears to more commonly determine when and on what the fish feed in a given body of water.

Water alkalinity, or the lack of it, influences the degree of competition for food among game fish. In fertile, highly productive lakes there is less competition between the game fish for the available food than in water containing minimal food supplies. There is so much food in some rich lakes that the fish could theoretically feed on any one of a dozen or more organisms at any given moment. In an alkaline lake the fish may abound in great numbers and reach lunker proportions within a two- or three-year span. In fact, in certain lakes, the fish become so fat and lazy you practically have to retrieve your flies into their mouths to arouse their desire to feed.

In lakes where the competition is great for a limited number of food organisms individual game fish are more aggressive. A wide variety of food types seems to attract their interest at any given moment. In addition, the feeding patterns of game fish in neutral or soft-water lakes tend to be less sporadic than in rich, alkaline waters. Soft-water lakes are incapable of producing the gross bulk of fish food per acre that hard-water lakes produce. As a result, their fish populations are "on the prod" for food more often and frequently less choosy about what they eat. At many excellent lakes, where surface feeding activity is usually limited to brief periods of insect hatching in the spring and fall, fish can be caught virtually anytime by simply trolling around the shoals and bays with a nymph resembling a caddis pupa, mayfly nymph or dragonfly nymph.

The Key to Locating Fish

One of the fundamental truisms of nature that points to the location of game fish is that fish are intimately bound to their food sources. Find the food and you'll almost always find the fish. Fish food in most lakes really begins with minute plant and animal life forms called "plankton." Some of the plankters are microscopic in size. Others are large enough to observe with the naked eye (Fig. 7).

Animal plankton are a necessary food element of water, and are found in most lakes to varying degrees. They are the very basis of life for nymphs, minnows, young game fish and a multitude of aquatic animals that form the diet of larger game fish. Plankton anchor the food chain which irrevocably binds together the various plants and animals in lakes.

One of the more visible manifestations of plankton is the phenomenon called "bloom." Bloom is the product of rapid buildups of planktonic algae during the summer months. Buildups of animal

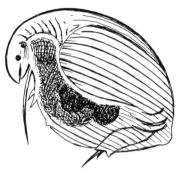

Fig. 7. *A plankter may be microscopic in size or may be large enough to be observed with the naked eye.*

plankton also take place, usually during the spring. A lake in bloom with vegetable-type plankton frequently takes on the appearance of a bowl of pea soup. Grayish or brown animal plankton is rarely so abundant.

Animal plankton forms (called "zooplankton" by biologists) not only feed the nymphs, forage fish and crustaceans that game fish feed upon, but also enter the adult game fishes' diets. It's not at all uncommon to dress a large fish and find the stomach crammed with a mass of plankton animals like water-fleas (*cladocera*).

Animal plankton tend to feed on vegetable plankton at varying depths in lakes. Forage fish and small game fish are attracted to the animal plankton. The concentrations of small fish in turn attract the larger, predatory fish. As a result, our ability to locate game fish in certain plankton-rich lakes is directly affected by the behavior of the minuscule animals.

Blooms of plant plankton (phytoplankton) sometimes influence

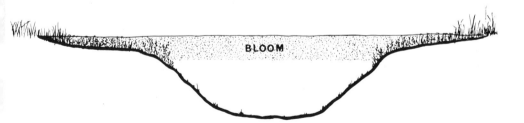

Fig. 8. *Lake "bloom" rarely extends beneath ten-foot depth.*

lake fly fishing methods in another way. Not too many anglers realize the bloom rarely extends in great density past a depth of ten feet (Fig. 8). The water under the souplike bloom is usually fairly clear and fishable by means of sinking fly lines. My fishing logs indicate dozens of occasions when this knowledge helped catch fish in blooming lakes by fishing nymphs and streamer flies on sinking lines.

More highly developed types of aquatic plant growth play host to scores of important fish foods and serve as protective cover for both game fish and forage fish. Frequently, predatory game fish, like northern pike, make use of weeds as cover from which to waylay other fish. One day I observed a large pike methodically squirming backwards into the weeds bordering a floating muskeg island. After about five minutes of writhing around he'd effectively concealed himself from sight and lay motionless. I was fascinated by the performance and watched while he darted out and engulfed a smaller pike, soon returning to his reedy lair. When the big pike had once again concealed his hulk in the weeds I waited a few minutes and cast near the spot, retrieving a streamer fly across his field of vision. The result was as you can well guess . . . a lunker that took his last swim in a skillet of hot lard!

Weed beds in three to 20 feet of water rank high on the list of prime fly fishing locations in lakes. Just how productive weed beds can be is exemplified by a five-day fishing trip on which three of us hooked and released 137 landlocked salmon on dry flies and nymphs from the vicinity of three weed beds, none of which exceeded 30 feet long and 10 feet wide! The fish inhabiting the food-producing weed bed areas are usually crammed with food. Certain weedy areas in rich, relatively alkaline lakes harbor a tremendous variety of food organisms, including damselfly and dragonfly nymphs, freshwater shrimps (scuds), snails, caddis larvae, water-fleas and forage fish.

The lake to which I just referred contains both landlocked salmon and brook trout. One morning when the surface of the lake was glassy smooth I counted 20 salmon and nine hefty brookies, from two to ten pounds apiece, clustered around a dark green weed bed which contrasted sharply against the whitish mud of the lake bottom. Later that same morning, when a light breeze ruffled the surface and a hatch of Black Drake mayfly duns materialized, I anchored my boat 60 feet or so upwind of the weed bed. Periodically, one of the salmon or brook trout would break the surface as it captured one of the hatching nymphs or drifting duns. Fishing with a dry, size 14 Black Quill, I hooked and released several of the high-jumping salmon and a three and a half pound brookie during the next two hours (Fig. 9).

Another extremely productive lake is set in a beautiful, pastoral valley surrounded by conifer-wooded hills. The bottom of this lake is saucer-shaped and, with the exception of an extensive mud flat at the south end, almost entirely carpeted with weed growth.

From one particular area on the southwest side of the lake phenomenal numbers of damselflies hatch in the late spring. It's tremendous fun fishing there with a fast-sinking fly line and size 10, 3XL damselfly nymphs when the husky rainbows and cutthroats are gorging on the naturals.

Fig. 9. *A landlocked salmon enjoys feeding on mayfly duns over a weed bed.*

Weed beds? I dream about the hundreds of delightful experiences I've enjoyed in the past 30 years of fly fishing lakes near concentrations of aquatic plants! There was that bright, sunny day on a small bass lake when, to my utter astonishment, virtually every cast with a Bucktail Coachman among the lily pads was met with a determined strike . . . an evening when two of us caught eight large bass on size 14 Blue Dun dry flies from over a submerged weedbed . . . the time when Fenton Roskelley and I literally dragged size 6 shrimp flies through the weeds at the lake bottom and caught a half-dozen brook trout over two pounds apiece! And, incidentally, those brookies were so crammed full of snails the shells rattled when we grasped the fish to remove our flies from their mouths! And, how could I ever forget the time when a friend and I chanced on a large school of walleyes prowling near the surface over an extensive weed bed, doing their darndest to drastically reduce the numbers of a school of forage fish which, in turn, were avidly gobbling up small black midges from the surface?

Other Productive Locations

Although we've devoted considerable space to a discussion of the attractiveness of pondweeds to game fish, weedy areas are only a few of the numerous parts of lakes where game fish can be found seeking food.

Gravel and silt beds in some lakes provide the growing places for certain varieties of mayfly nymphs, caddis fly larvae, midge larvae and mollusks not generally associated with weedy areas.

In some large, rocky lakes lacking extensive weedy shallows, the gravel, rocks and silt near shore or on shoals are prime feeding stations for the gamefish populations. Some of the more important lake-inhabiting mayflies, like the march brown, hatch from such hard-bottom lake regions.

In addition to the fish food production some hard lake bottoms provide, lakeshore gravel serves as spawning beds for certain species of game fish during the appropriate seasons. Some of the largest trout caught from lakes on flies are hooked during the spring months when the big ones are cruising the gravel and rocky shorelines intent on reproduction. The spawning urge concentrates mature trout for a brief time in areas where they're relatively easy pickin's for fly fishermen. Members of the fly fishing fraternity unfamiliar with lake fishing may tend to scoff at the prospects of casting hook-filled feathery bouquets into the boudoirs of female trout. However, it's hard to deny the fascination connected with hooking and releasing trout from two to 15 pounds! Spawning trout are usually sad table fare at best, but it's difficult to condemn a man who hooks and releases spawning fish for purely sporting purposes.

Rocky shores and shoals in certain lakes provide fly fishing opportunities of a high order. In early spring and late fall, lake trout, for example, desert the extreme depths they tend to frequent during the summer and for brief periods can be found within a few feet of the surface. Lakers can be taken readily on flies when they're in shallow water. Another salmonoid that sometimes feeds around rocky shallows is the Kamloops strain of the rainbow trout. Kamloops trout, as they're called almost universally, are found mostly in lakes in British Columbia and the northern panhandle region of the state of Idaho. The Kamloops is a voracious predator of other fishes. An abundance of kokanee salmon are responsible for the big 'bows attaining world record proportions in Pend Oreille (Pon-der-ay') Lake, Idaho. Until these high-jumping tackle-busters attain sufficient size to feed on other fish their diets consist mostly of plankton, insect larvae, leeches and small minnows.

Underwater obstructions are also prime places to seek out game fish in lakes. There's something about the sight of a submerged tree or underwater brush pile that makes the hair on one's neck snap to attention. If there were any hair on my head it would probably behave the same way. Perhaps it's the knowledge that somewhere in those dark and mysterious looking recesses, or buried deep amongst that frightening tangle of snags lurks a lunker bass, pike, trout or school of crappies.

Why do fish favor such places? Both forage fish and certain aquatic insects usually favor locations that provide good cover. Game fish themselves will lurk in the protective shadows cast by the limbs of sunken trees or brush and lie motionless, waiting for some unsuspecting minnow to stray from cover.

Some of the best lake fly fishing will be found at the bases of submerged brush piles in stump-ranch-type lakes and at the mouths of inlet streams. I've had eight- to 15-pound test tippets parted in such locations as a result of trying to put the brakes to outsized brookies

Fig. 10. *Excellent lake fly fishing can be found in stump-ranch-type lakes, which typically have cover as above.*

and pike. Once at a favorite stump-ranch lake (Fig. 10), a two-foot-plus rainbow pounced on my gray fur nymph the minute it hit the water near a submerged brush pile and churned wildly off through the staghornlike maze! The huge trout suddenly changed direction to the left, doubled back and half-hitched my tippet around another snag as he took to the air in a gloriously spectacular broadside jump! The fish broke off instantly! It was a half hour before I'd calmed down enough to tie on another fly. The deep-bodied rainbow appeared to be in the eight-pound class.

On another trip to the same lake my companion hooked an immense brook trout. As luck would have it, he just happened to be fishing his bucktail fly on a tippet testing four pounds.

"I'll never land him on this tippet!" groaned my chum hopelessly as the monster brookie (which we estimated to weigh five or six pounds) sawed back and forth through weeds and brush piles, shaking its head determinedly.

He didn't! The brookie finally swam into the nightmarish entanglement of roots beneath a floating island and broke off. Since that day neither of us fish that lake with a tippet testing less than six pounds. Most of the time we use eight-pound tippet there.

The mouths of inlet and outlet streams to flowage lakes are excellent locations to seek fish with flies (Fig. 11). The cool, well oxygenated flow from an inlet stream seems to attract both game fishes and the organisms they feed upon, especially during the midsummer warm-water period.

Factors other than water temperature also attract fish to the areas where inlets flow into lakes. Terrestrial insects are frequently carried into the lakes by streams. And, the action of the streams' currents sometimes forms channels in the sand, silt or gravel adjacent to the inlet—channels where hungry fish lie in wait for easy pickin's. During their annual spawning runs, forage fish, like smelt and kokanee salmon, school up in large numbers along the shorelines and at the

Fig. 11. *One area where fish can often be hooked is around the mouths of inlet/outlet streams.*

mouths of streams. The heavy concentrations of forage fish are almost certain to attract predatory sport fish like landlocked salmon, trout, walleyes, crappies, bass and pike.

At other times, in lakes where the inlets serve as spawning streams for migratory fish like salmon, immature smolts returning to the lake attract predatory game fish to the scene at specific times each year. When significant numbers of smolts swim into a lake from an inlet stream it serves as an unusually fine opportunity for fly fishermen to catch large sport fishes like trout, landlocked salmon and northern pike on streamer flies resembling small fishes.

Arctic grayling and most other species of salmonoid fish are well known for their tendencies to feed where streams enter lakes. Really large grayling, from two to five pounds, frequently feed at both inlet and outlet areas in lakes.

Bass and Pike Seek Cover

Most pike, bass and panfish devotees are keenly aware of the angling possibilities afforded by lily pads in lakes. The distinctive, flat-leafed water plants are found in both hard- and soft-water lakes. Lily pads serve as excellent protective cover and feeding stations for game fish. The pads usually abound with terrestrial and aquatic life like frogs, nymphs, leeches, snails and forage fish. Nymphs of aquatic insects crawl up the underwater portions of lily pad stems to hatch into their adult forms on the roundish, flat leaves.

Very precise casting is usually required to fish lily pad areas in an effective manner. Because of the accuracy necessary to drop a bass bug in a small pocket in dense pad growths it's usually more productive to alternate fishing and boat handling with your companion. One man will fish for say 20 minutes, then the other angler will take over the fly rod for a similar amount of time.

Holes

Earlier in this chapter we talked about how inlet streams sometimes carve depressions in lake floors. Such eroded places in the lake bottom often host very large individual game fish. Long, relatively narrow channels between or within the confines of weed beds serve similarly to attract outsized individual game fish. Both the lake floor

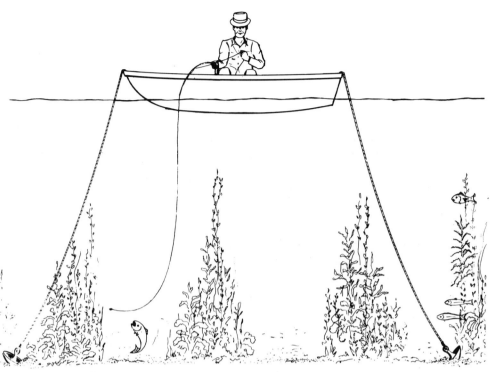

Fig. 12.   *The long, narrow channels among weed beds at the lake bottom offer prime fishing prospects.*

depressions and the channels among the weed beds are commonly called "holes" by lake fishermen and are ideally suited to deeply sunken nymphs, wet flies, bucktails and streamers (Fig. 12).

Why holes attract the "big ones" should be self-evident, based upon what's already been said about the lake environment. Solitary old tackle-busters usually are as lazy as they are large. Lake floor depressions afford them excellent protective cover by breaking their body silhouettes. And, the weedy channel areas are frequently aquatic cornucopias, crawling with the nymphs, larvae and crustaceans fish gorge on.

In a discussion of lake fishing methods with other anglers conversation inevitably turns to springs that percolate water through the bottom of the lake. If you can find them, springs are exceptional lake areas to fly fish. They attract fish when surrounding lake waters are excessively warm during the summer months and promote the growth of certain pondweeds which, in turn, produce aquatic animals that attract fish.

But, locating a submerged spring in a lake is no simple task. Even when you employ an angler's thermometer properly, the odds are great that most of the "springs" you locate will turn out to be either the middle or bottom layer of water. The best chances of locating real springs are in relatively shallow, unstratified lakes and ponds, where one's judgment won't be fooled by the cooler temperature-oxygen layers. There are a number of such springs in a small, heavily fished lake not far from my home where, despite the heavy angling pressure, knowledgeable fly fishermen each season hook numerous trout in the two- to seven-pound class.

Thus far, our discussion has centered mostly on the lakes themselves, plants that grow in them and general locations where fish are most likely to be found. However, in order to catch fish from lakes on artificial flies with any degree of consistency, it's helpful to understand some of the particulars in the life cycles and habits of the creatures fish eat.

Lake Species Enjoy Varied Diet

Lake-bound game fish engulf an astounding variety of aquatic and terrestrial life. We examined earlier the dependency of most aquatic life on those microscopic plants and animals called plankton. Fish of all sizes and most species consume considerable quantities of animal plankton, while numerous other aquatic animals, including insect nymphs, also eat the plankters

Some game fish consume common mollusks like snails and fresh-water clams. Snails are generally found in water ranging from one to six feet deep where their foods, the algae and other aquatic plants abound. They travel over the bottoms of lakes, climb plant stems and glide along the underside of the surface film. Brook trout are especially noted for their tendency to gorge on snails. I've personally counted nearly three dozen snails in the stomach of a single, five-pound brookie!

Leeches are another aquatic dish favored by most lake game fish, including bass, trout and crappies. Leeches seem to be most numerous in lakes containing a lot of bottom debris and in places where there is an abundance of dead, organic material.

Streamer flies tied to represent these blood-sucking, aquatic annelids are usually effective fish getters in most parts of the United States. My own leech creation, which has no name as yet, is tied on a size 6, 4XL hook. The inch-long tail consists of a bunch of fluffy, brown olive marabou feathers. The body is tied full and tapered out of soft, spun, dun gray rabbit fur, topped by an overbody of brown olive marabou and ribbed with fine, oval silver tinsel. The fly has a short, collarlike hackle tied out of brown olive marabou. An effective variation of the design is tied in identical fashion using black marabou and magenta spun fur. The fly, which I designed for a specific lake, has proved just about equally effective on rainbow, brook trout, bass and panfish.

Forage fish and the young of virtually every species of freshwater game fish ultimately find themselves under consideration as possible main courses on the dinner menus of adult fish. Nowhere in nature is the old saw about how "the big fish eat the little fish" more true than in this fundamental aquatic relationship. Even the several insectivorous strains of cutthroat trout native to western waters are known to resort to a kind of cannibalism when the opportunities present themselves.

Some of the more common fishes which anglers suggest with streamer flies in lakes are the shiners, madtoms, sculpins, sunfishes and trout fingerlings. (Fig. 13).

Terrestrial insects and small animals also enter gamefish diets. Land-inhabiting insects, like grasshoppers, crickets, bees, ants and spiders, are frequently blown by the wind, hop or fly into the water. In some areas of the country tremendous mating flights of flying ants periodically descend on lakes. Such ant flights occur sporadically throughout late May and early June where I live in northeastern Washington.

I recall one day in particular when I was nymph fishing. A dense algal bloom forced me to fish by artificials on a fast-sinking line. It was one of those infectiously lazy warm late spring afternoons when the fish were so heavily gorged on natural damselfly nymphs that my artificials aroused little more than passive interest on the part of the fish. I had quit fishing after lunch to relax and doze in the sun when I suddenly became aware of the sound of surface feeding. A mating flight of large black ants with amber wings had descended onto the water. Within minutes the pea-soup colored pond was rippling with hundreds of feeding fish. I changed from my fast-sinking fly line to a floater and tied a size 10 black ant imitation to the tippet. The action was fast and furious!

Fig. 13 *Common Lake Minnows, Forage Fish, Gamefish Fingerlings & Patterns to Simulate Them*

Species	Where Found	Basic Colors	Artificials
Alewife (*Alosa psudoharengus*)	NE, UMW, SE.	Back gray blue green. Sides silver. Dark spot on shoulder.	blue/green/white Coho Fly
American Smelt (*Osmerus mordax*)	NE, UMW, SE.	Back olive. Sides silvery. Large scales. Pearly gill covers. Brown forked tail.	Nine-Three Ballou Special Jane Craig
Bluntnose Minnow (*Pimephales notatus*)	NE, MW, SW, S, W.	Back pale olive. Sides silver blue. Dark band entire length. Black spot base of tail.	Supervisor
Brook Silverside Minnow (*Labidsesthes sicculus*)	NE, LMW, S, N.	Slender. Semitransparent. Pale green. Violet gill plates. Silver lateral line. Large eyes.	Silver Shiner
Brook Trout Fingerling (*Salvelinus fontinalus*)	Most of USA.	Back green black. Sides creamy orange. Speckled.	Little Brook Trout Bucktail Brook Trout Streamer
Brown Trout Fingerling (*Salmo trutta*)	Most of USA.	Back black brown. Sides brown shading to creamy belly. Red and yellow speckles.	Little Brown Trout Bucktail
Fallfish (*Semotilus corporalis*)	NE, SE.	Back brown olive. Sides silver rosy hue.	Gray Ghost
Golden Shiner (*Notemigonus crysoleucas*)	NE, MS, S, W.	Back dark brown to olive. Sides gold.	Golden Shiner Streamer Golden Shiner Bucktail Yellow & White Bucktail
Horned Dace (*Semotilus atromaculatus*)	NE, NW, W, S, SW.	Similar to Fallfish with black mark at base of first three dorsal fin rays. Barbels upper jaw.	Gray Ghost
Kokanee (landlocked sockeye salmon) (*Oncorhynchus nerka*)	W, NW, NE.	Back dark blue black. Sides silver.	Blue/White Coho Fly, Blue/Green/ White Coho Fly Blue/Red White Coho Fly
Mottled Sculpin (*Cottus bairdi*)	NW, NE.	Back dark mottled brown black. Sides mottled brown. Black vertical bar at base of tail.	Muddler Minnow Spuddler
Perch Fry Fingerling	Most of USA.	Back dark green. Sides pale greenish. Belly whitish.	Marabou Perch Rex's Perch Fry Bucktail
Rainbow Fingerling (*Salmo irridius*)	Most of USA.	Back dark green. Sides shade to pink with white belly.	Little Rainbow Bucktail
Satin Fin (*Notropis whipplii*)	NE mostly.	Overall blue purple with yellow fins.	Satin Fin Streamer
Tadpole Madtom (*Noturus gyrinus*)	NE, SE mostly.	Back dark brown. Sides brown gray. Belly white.	Mad Tom Marabou Muddler Minnow

Midges: Bread 'n' Butter Insects

In some regions of the country midges are far more important as food for lake fish than mayflies, on a year-round basis. Midges (Order: *diptera*) in their pupal and larval forms are found from extreme shallows to depths exceeding 30 feet, and fish don't appear to be choosy about where they feed on them. Lake game fish of many species are known to gobble up midge larvae from the bottom, the pupae during their ascent to the surface and midge adults from the surface film itself. Midges hatch periodically throughout the year, peak periods coming in the spring and fall months in temperate zone waters.

Midge larvae are generally found in large numbers in lakes with soft, silty bottoms. One fisheries biologist told me that no other insect is so important as a food item for so wide a variety of fishes. The larvae and pupae of midges are cylindrical and wormlike in shape and are found in a variety of colors, including red, cream and green. Adult, pupal and larval midges all can be effectively suggested with artificial flies on hook sizes varying from 26 to 10 (Fig. 14). Midges and certain other important fish foods will be discussed in greater detail in the chapters dealing with specific angling methods. But, for now let's continue to strive for an understandable overview of the lake environment.

Mayflies and their nymphs are the most publicized natural game-fish foods. The nymphs are readily identified by their two or three tails, the gills on their backs and sides and the single claw on each foot (Fig. 15). Although some species of mayflies are found as nymphs in silt, around debris or near weeds, other varieties common to lakes inhabit relatively rocky, hard lake bottoms like those along rocky shorelines and shoals.

Some of the most consistently productive mayfly nymph artificials for lake fishing are tied with soft, furry looking bodies suggesting the fuzzy gill filaments of the naturals.

Adult mayflies (Order: *ephemeroptera*) are usually beautiful, delicate-winged creatures that can be recognized by their two pairs of wings (the rear set is considerably shorter than the front) resting in a saillike position over their backs when at rest. Adult mayflies have either two or three fairly long tails.

Unlike midges, mayflies undergo a gradual, incomplete metamor-

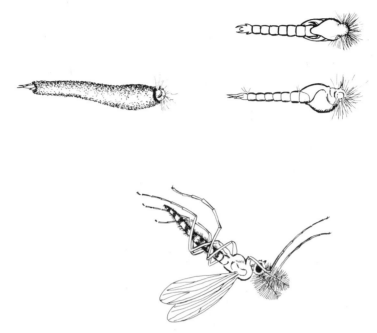

Fig. 14. *A midge, typical of the breed that provides a good part of the fish diet in many lakes.*

Fig. 15. *Mayfly nymphs are the early stage of this ubiquitous insect.*

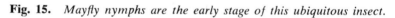

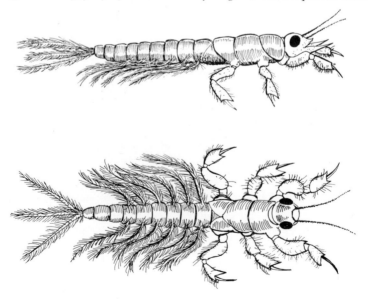

phosis from underwater forms into adult insects. They hatch from eggs into nymphs which develop gradually until hatching time when the nymphal cases break open and release the first of two adult stages called the "dun" (Fig. 16). Duns have short tails and are usually found drying their wings on the surface of the lake, on shoreline rocks and plants or flying away from the lake towards the shore.

The final stage of the adult mayfly is called the "spinner" and results from the dun shedding its skin. Spinner mayflies usually have glassier wings than duns, more colorful and distinct body and tail markings and longer tails (Fig. 17). Spinners are usually seen flying towards the lake from the shore as the time for egg laying approaches.

Fig. 16. *Mayfly duns are the first adult stage of this insect.*

Fig. 17. *When the Mayfly dun sheds its skin, the adult spinner is released.*

Mayflies lay their eggs on or beneath the surface, then fall spent on the surface film and die. Famous dry flies, like the Adams, are sometimes dressed with "spent" wings to suggest the dead spinners lying on the water. Most game fish feed avidly on mayflies in both their underwater and adult forms.

Grayling, trout, bass, sunfish and landlocked salmon all usually enjoy a field day when duns hatch and spinners descend on lakes to fulfill their brief destinies. Usually, the most productive dry fly fishing occurs during the early part of a dun hatch and early in a spinner flight, before the water becomes so littered with insects an artificial gets lost in the crowd. At the end of hatches and spinner flights the fish usually become so gorged that they lose interest in further feeding.

Anglers in some parts of the country refer to virtually any small insect that wends its way to the lake's surface as a "spinner." To do so with regard to any insect other than a mayfly is a display of gross ignorance, pardonable only by another fly fisherman!

Peak hatching periods for mayflies occur in the late spring and early summer across most of the northern United States and Canada, with some activity continuing intermittently throughout the summer and fall months. A complete text would be required to outline the identities and hatching peculiarities of the hundreds of mayfly species in North America. From an angler's standpoint such detail is unnecessary. If you take careful note of the mayflies that hatch throughout the season on the waters you fish, you'll be able to represent most of them at the fly tying vise with little trouble. On the other hand, if you are a complete neophyte at fly fishing or unfamiliar with the mayfly hatches of your region, here's a selection of standard American patterns that will serve as starters virtually anywhere: Royal Coachman, Adams, Black Quill, Light Hendrickson, Dark Hendrickson, Light Cahill, Dark Cahill, Ginger Quill, Blue Dun, Pale Sulphery Dun, Olive Dun, White Miller and Grizzly Wulff. (See Chapter 11.)

Dragonflies and their close cousins the delicate damselflies (both, Order: *odonata*) are probably the two aquatic insects most confused by fly fishermen. Both are terrifically important as fish food organisms. The relatively large dragonfly nymphs are avidly sought by most of the trout, bass and panfish. Damselfly nymphs are smaller than dragonfly nymphs (Fig. 18), but no less eagerly accepted as food by most game fish.

Fig. 18. *The dragonfly nymph (above) is larger than the damselfly nymph.*

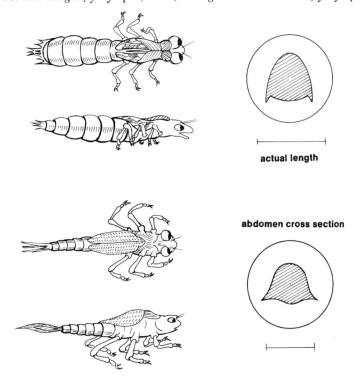

actual length

abdomen cross section

Like mayflies, both dragonflies and damselflies undergo a gradual incomplete metamorphic development from egg to adult. Their nymphs undergo a series of "instars," or developmental stages, before finally hatching into adult insects.

The nymphs of both insects are fiercely predatory creatures. Dragonfly nymphs are usually observed sprawled on or among weeds, silt and trashy litter at the bottoms of lakes. They amble slowly and methodically along hunting small fish and insect nymphs, larvae and pupae. But, once they elect to move rapidly, they are capable of darting about with great speed by forcibly expelling water from their tracheal chambers. The "stripping" retrieve described in Chapter 4 is one highly effective means of emulating the darting movements of dragonfly nymphs through the water.

Dragonfly nymphs vary in size from one-half inch to about two inches long. They can be positively identified by the hinged hooks on the lower halves of their mouth parts as well as by their relatively large size and distinctive shapes. The fast-flying adult dragonflies are relatively unimportant to fly fishermen. Their rapid flight foils the efforts of most game fish to pick them out of the air.

Damselfly nymphs are slender, inch-long, roundish nymphs with three appendages resembling paddle blades at their hind ends. The appendages are actually the nymphs' gills, which they employ in much the same way a skindiver uses swim fins. The nymphs of most lake species live around aquatic vegetation, and vary in color from pale tan to light olive green.

Adult damselflies are smaller in most cases and more delicate in appearance than dragonfly adults. At rest, damselflies hold their wings over their backs, unlike their rigid-winged cousins. The bodies of adult damselflies are very slender and usually colored blue, gray, green or grayish black. Damselfly flight is weak and hovering in contrast to the strong, rapid flight of dragonflies. Adult damsels usually appear in the largest numbers in the late spring. They're frequently spotted flying erratically near weeds and lily pads where they present easy targets for game fish fast and strong enough to leap into the air and pick them off. Some of the most frustrating moments of fly fishing lakes occur when fish are picking damselfly adults from the air *above* the surface of the water. More about that later.

Caddis flies (Order: *trichoptera*), known as "sedges" in parts of

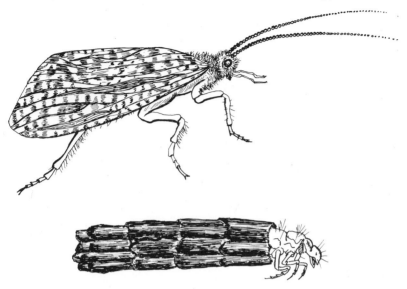

Fig. 19. *The Caddis fly's life cycle is closer to that of the midge than to that of the dragonfly, mayfly, or damselfly.*

Canada, are among the aquatic insects most avidly sought by game fish. The life cycle of the caddis more closely resembles that of the midges and mosquitoes than of the mayfly, damselfly and dragonfly. Caddis flies start out as eggs, which hatch into larvae. Eventually, the caddis larva constructs a pupa or cocoon around itself. Inside the cocoon the larval worm reorganizes itself into an adult insect.

Caddis fly larvae construct their pupal homes from a wide variety of underwater building materials like sticks, sand and rubble, or by weaving netlike structures around themselves somewhat in the manner of silk worms (Fig. 19). The famous "Strawman Nymph" was tied to represent a cased, carpenter-type caddis pupa. The immensely popular "Carey Special" wet fly, used mostly in the western United States and British Columbia, and the "Big Ugly" nymph, also of Canadian origin, are tied to resemble caddis pupae rising to the surface to hatch.

Adult caddis flies are usually nocturnal, drab colored insects varying in size from hook sizes 18 to 6. They hold their fuzzy wings tentlike over their backs at rest and their flight is usually erratic and dancing. Caddis flies have long, threadlike antennae and no tails.

What is probably some of the most exciting lake dry fly fishing in North America erupts late in June on certain lakes in the British Columbia interior when large caddis flies called "traveling sedges" begin to hatch in numbers.

The slab-sided, high-jumping Kamloops trout inhabiting those lakes feed actively on the sedges in both their underwater and adult forms. During hatches of traveling sedges experienced local anglers cast large dry flies and sometimes skitter them on the surface in ways that emulate the wakes left by the naturals as they scamper along the surface film.

A friend once had the surprise of a lifetime when he accidentally hooked what appeared to be about a ten-pound Kamloops while rowing ashore during a pelting rainstorm. He allowed his fly to trail in the water behind the boat while pulling on the oars. The dragging fly made a V on the surface, rather like the scurrying of a sedge.

Suddenly, there was a tremendous splash where his dry fly had been. Out of the water in a towering somersault charged a gorgeous, silvery fish in the 30-inch class! Frantic in its efforts to escape the bite of the barb and the pull of the line the rainbow ripped line from his reel at incredible speed. After 20 minutes the battling Kamloops began to show signs of tiring. "I may land him," grunted my pal, half to himself. Then, the line went slack. The trout was gone, probably as a result of the hook wearing a hole in its mouth during the prolonged tussle.

Caddis flies usually hatch late in the evening over shoals, silt and weed beds, or lake bottom regions strewn with rubble. A usual caddis fly hatch is of short duration, rarely lasting more than an hour and a half. Sometimes the hatching period is incredibly brief, like the time a friend hooked a landlocked salmon at the beginning of a hatch, fought the fish for ten minutes, and discovered to his utter dismay that the hatch had ended by the time the fish came to the net.

Crustaceans Grow 'em Big 'n' Fat

Biologists tell us trout and other game fish feed mostly on plankton and aquatic insects until they reach the size where it's essential for them to take in food forms of greater nutritive value in order to attain additional growth. Aquatic crustaceans are one form of fish food capable of producing rapid growth in game fish. Some of those crustaceans can be effectively represented at the fly tying bench.

There are two main types of freshwater crustaceans. The larger varieties include the crayfish, sow bugs and scuds, sometimes called freshwater shrimps. Smaller forms include the fairy shrimps, water-fleas and a wide assortment of additional aquatic animals too numerous to chronicle here. Scuds and crayfish are the easiest to imitate with artificial flies.

Scuds vary from less than a quarter of an inch to over an inch long (Fig. 20). They are aquatic plant eaters and are found among numerous pondweed types. In shape scuds resemble tiny saltwater shrimps to a degree, but their bodies are narrower and their backs

Fig. 20.   *Scud, or freshwater shrimp, are fairly easy to imitate with artificial flies.*

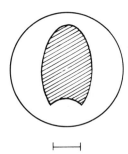

arched rather like fleas. Scuds come in many colors, from yellowish green to almost black.

American lake anglers have devised many effective wet fly patterns in their attempts to recreate scuds on fly hooks. Ted Trueblood's "Otter Nymph" is one of the best. The pattern incorporates a dubbed mixture of silky otter and glistening seal furs which imparts to the fly a suggestion of the semitranslucency of a living scud. The fur is usually picked out underneath the body of this fly to simulate the gill-feet of the natural crustacean.

Other fish-killing shrimp flies are dressed in a "shell-back" design with overbodies tied out of deer body hair, goose and turkey wing feather sections. The bodies of most of these patterns are usually wrapped out of chenille or floss and palmered with varying shades of hackle to resemble gill-feet, like my friend Gil Nyerges' "Nyerges Nymph," which is a highly effective artificial scud. The "Otter Nymph" is included in the chapter containing fly dressings (Chapter 11).

Scuds have the ability to climb, swim, glide or jump in the water. As a result of their multiplicity of physical antics a wide variety of retrieves can be employed to suggest their underwater movements.

Another crustacean most good-sized game fish can't resist is the crayfish, known in some areas as a "crawdad" or "crawdaddy." Both bass and trout are fond of them. Contrary to common belief, most large game fish will eat crayfish in both their soft-shelled and hard-shelled phases. Crayfish shed their skins periodically as they grow larger. Before their new skins harden they're especially vulnerable to predation and easy pickin's for virtually any fish large enough to swallow such a hefty morsel.

During daytime hours crayfish usually conceal themselves among the submerged rocks and rubble along the shore and at the lake bottom, venturing forth from their hide-aways anytime from late afternoon to after sunset. When you're dead set on catching a truly red-fleshed, large trout or a few flavorful smallmouth bass for the table, work large wet flies and nymphs over rock ledges and shoals from dusk to nearly midnight.

Impact of Water Temperature

Water temperature not only influences the probable locations of game fish on a seasonal basis, but also affects the availability of natural fish foods during their complex seasonal cycles.

To begin with, let's forget for the moment that there is such a thing as "opening day" of fishing season. A lot of good lake areas in regions experiencing mild winters have certain waters open to angling the year around or on winter-only seasons. Quite a few anglers can fly fish lakes practically 12 months out of the year. Fish eat throughout the entire year, and we shouldn't forget it!

We've already examined how plankton multiply rapidly during the spring and summer months and provide food for both game fish and other aquatic animals. Water temperature also affects the sexual activity and physical growth of aquatic insects, crustaceans and forage fish. And, gamefish activity is intimately bound to that of the organisms on which they feed.

For example, it's fairly common knowledge that when a fish's metabolic rate is appreciably slowed by the effects of cold water, its feeding, sexual activity and physical movements are similarly affected. In the case of most cold-water species this slowing down of the rate of the living processes usually occurs when the water temperatures fall much below 45° F. Maximum trout activity normally takes place between 47 and 65° F, within which range the most abundant insect hatches occur. In northern temperate zones this is the water temperature range of spring and early fall.

In the case of deep lakes, once the water temperatures in food shelf areas soar past the limits where food organisms are abundant and active, and the water is uncomfortable to the species preferring cooler climes, it's only natural for the fish to gravitate towards deeper, cooler waters where other types of foods may be available to them. This same principle applies in varying degrees to deep lakes containing some of the warm-water species.

In shallow lakes, where no escape from warming waters is possible, the game fish sometimes experience a repression of their body functions similar to that they experience during extreme cold-water periods.

Fly fishing methods are similarly influenced. Choice of potentially effective artificials, the speeds to retrieve them and the depth to fish all hinge ultimately on water temperature's effects on fish and fish foods.

During the very warm and frigidly cold-water periods of summer and midwinter, when the game fish are feeding mostly on forage fish, nymphs, mollusks and crustaceans, and when the physical life processes of the fish and their foods are slowed markedly, fly fishermen are forced to employ methods which effectively match the lack of the hatch. Sinking fly lines; slow retrieves; thorough combing of likely water; nymph, shrimp and streamer flies are the major weapons in our continuing skirmishes with lake game fish in cold water.

When water temperatures approach the range promoting insect hatches and injecting fish with vitality, one is compelled to play a three-dimensional game of chance with the fish, employing lines, retrieves and fly patterns effective from the surface on down to the bottom.

Competition Between Species Affects Fishing

Additional factors affect our reading of the cryptic book of lakes. One of the most important is whether or not a lake is inhabited by a single species of game fish or shares it with other fish species. For example, when certain strains of cutthroat trout exist exclusively in a lake—without competition for food from other fishes—they'll usually be found virtually anywhere in that lake where food is abundant. However, introduce a second species of game fish, like rainbow trout or bluegill sunfish, and a keen competition arises between the two species for the same food supply.

In this specific case, the antisocial cutthroat trout usually refuse to compete for food with other species. Rainbows or bluegills would soon take over most of the best feeding areas in the shallow parts of the lake. The cutthroats would fade away to deeper areas and tend to subsist mostly on a diet of water-fleas, midges and other deep-water organisms, venturing into the shallows only when a superabundance of feed reduced the competition.

Brown trout, brook trout and rainbows seem to share feeding water more amicably than cutthroats. Brookies do most of their heavy feeding near or at the lake bottom. Rainbow trout and browns feed at all levels of lakes. All three are more aggressive and predatory than the insectivorous strains of cutthroat trout.

Lake trout, walleyes, muskies, bass and northern pike depend heavily on other fish for their food supplies. All five species require forage fish as primary diet. And, all will coexist in the same lake with one or more species of game fish, provided their feeding areas don't greatly overlap. There are numerous lakes in the United States and Canada where the shallows are inhabited almost solely by pike and walleyes and the deep expanses by lake trout. Unlike the insectivorous cutthroats, the lake trout is a fish accommodating best to waters in the 45-degree range, which even in the northlands lie at considerable depths during the summer months. By nature a deep-water creature, the lake trout's brief shallow escapades occur mostly in the early spring and again in the late fall when near-surface temperatures are agreeable to him or the urge to spawn attracts him to the shoals.

There are many lakes across this country and in Canada where good fly fishing can be had for mixed gamefish species. From our standpoint as fly fishermen it's essential to know if a given lake contains several gamefish species and if so, what they might be. That information influences all the other factors thus far discussed.

Some of the best mixed species lakes are impoundments along the TVA system and reservoirs in western states. All such bodies of water do not offer good fishing possibilities, however. Fishing prospects diminish drastically when the managing authorities manipulate the lakes' water levels like yo-yos, suddenly injecting excessively cold waters into the lakes when fish are spawning or drawing lake levels down far enough to leave fertilized gamefish eggs high and dry on the beach.

Reservoirs Offer Opportunities

Let's take a brief look at the angling opportunities of a typical reservoir containing several sport fish species. The 11,000-acre lake we'll discuss is one of several federally constructed catch basins in its region which receive the agricultural run-off waters from an irrigation project.

The reservoir has some relatively deep portions, but at least half of the lake consists of shallow channels and bays that wind tortuously among hundreds of sand dune islands. Fed by creeks and wasteways which funnel water off adjacent sugar beet and corn fields, it also has an outlet and can be considered a true flowage lake. It is open to sport fishing for all its gamefish species the year around.

During the months of January, February and March, several weedy bays with sand and gravel bottoms, plus an extensive, narrow arm of the lake, provide area anglers with plenty of opportunities to fly fish for perch, crappies and rainbow trout.

With the advent of spring, the major creek inlet channel and other favorable portions of the island-studded end of the lake offer excellent largemouth bass fishing. Some of the wasteway streams kick out flurries of good trout fishing.

As the waters warm in the late spring, bluegills school near the willow-lined shores and the trout in the main portions of the lake show increasing signs of sexual activity. Because of the reservoir's great size and fairly constant levels, as well as the productive nature of the water itself, the fishing in the reservoir is fairly consistent from year to year.

The state's game department, one of the earliest pioneers in the techniques of chemical lake rehabilitation, realized that the reservoir was far too extensive and complicated a drainage to manage on a single species basis. Chemical rehabilitation, as it's practical today, is best suited to smaller lakes. Because the lake's warm-water fishes (the perch, crappies and bass) take good care of their own reproduction, all the game department fish managers really had to do to create a fine, mixed-species fishing lake was to annually sweeten the pot with several thousand legal-sized rainbow trout. The lake's abundant food supply did the rest.

As one might conclude, a few fly fishermen soon discovered the willingness of the reservoir trout, bass and panfish to take flies. It is a classic example of how fishing opportunity was created where little more than a desert existed previously.

Waters like this can be found in various parts of the United States. As moving waterways decrease, such man-made reservoirs will re-

Fig. 21. *A fly fisherman's mixed bag catch from a reservoir: crappies, perch, trout and bluegill.*

Fig. 22. *The thousands of lakes in the far north of Canada offer virtually untapped opportunities for the fly fisherman.*

ceive more and more attention from fly fishermen. They can provide rewarding action (Fig. 21).

The countless lakes in the now wildly primitive Canadian Shield offer additional hope for tomorrow's fly fishermen. In some, it's possible to catch arctic grayling of trophy proportions (two to five pounds), walleyes, lake trout and northern pike on flies—all in the course of a single day! (Fig. 22.)

In that rocky, lonely northern vastness you'll encounter two basic types of lakes: seepage waters of varying size containing a single species of game fish, and immense, meandering flowage lakes joined together by complex river systems. The flowage lakes usually contain several sport fish species.

One of the very best northern fishing areas centers at 17-mile-long Waterbury Lake, a part of the McKenzie River drainage system. Waterbury lies 210 air-miles north of the village of Lac La Ronge, Saskatchewan, in a more or less straight line between 89-mile-long Wollaston Lake and that 3,050-square mile freshwater "sea" named

Lake Athabasca. Waterbury Lake is accessible only by float plane during the summer months.

Best known to midwestern anglers as a reliable lake to cast or troll for lake trout up to 30 pounds, Waterbury also has some lightly fished northern pike hang-outs and inlet and outlet streams containing trophy grayling. Smaller, nearby lakes contain northern pike and walleyes.

Two fine rivers greatly enhance the fly fishing opportunities at Waterbury Lake. The Hell River, smallest of the two, is an inlet of medium size by U.S. standards. The larger, Unknown River is the lake's major outlet stream flowing northward.

Both the Hell and Unknown rivers resemble drainage lakes more than streams. Quite a few similar far-northern rivers consist primarily of relatively long, narrow lakes connected by stretches of rapids varying in length from a few yards to more than a quarter of a mile.

The lake portions of both rivers contain mostly northern pike, while the rapids attract grayling. Lake areas immediately below the rapids often teem with large whitefish which, incidentally, come to dry flies beautifully!

During the course of a few minutes it's possible to stand where the rapids churn into the lake, catch grayling on dry flies in the moving water, change rods and hook pike on streamers or bass bugs in adjacent slack waters. Sometimes it isn't even necessary to change rods!

One day while fishing the Hell River with Ted Jackson of the Waterbury Lake camp, Ted latched onto a good-sized grayling that raced downstream into the eddying pool at the foot of a rapids. Almost immediately the grayling was victimized by a pike in the ten-pound class! Ted didn't land either fish. The pike's sharp teeth ended the scrap by slicing his leader. An hour later the same thing happened to me!

Up to this point our discussion concerning game fish themselves has been relatively general in content—generalities that give an all-important overview of the lake environment. But, each of the popular North American sport fishes displays specific characteristics of behavior that form a necessary part of the total understanding one needs to evolve effective fly fishing methods for them.

2

Important Lake Fish

Landlocked salmon (*Salmo salar sebago*) afford some of the most thrilling fly fishing opportunities in this hemisphere. This streamlined, silvery, high-jumper sometimes hits a streamer fly with the speed of a rocket, somersaulting time and again out of the water and engaging in high speed runs that make a fly reel scream wild melodies!

The average size of landlocked salmon varies between two and eight pounds in most lakes, but some larger fish are occasionally encountered by fly fishermen and trollers (Fig. 23). The general range of the landlocked salmon covers New England, the Canadian maritime provinces, Newfoundland, Labrador, the British Isles, Norway, Sweden and the Soviet Union.

Landlocked salmon usually spawn from sometime in October until the latter part of November. In the species' northern range spawning takes place earlier in the year.

As a young fish in the stream of its hatching, the "parr," or immature salmon, sustains itself on aquatic insects and small fishes. Adult salmon subsist primarily on freshwater smelt and other forage species.

Fig. 23. *Landlocked salmon come large in size and high in fighting power.*

However, in some lakes these beautiful, streamlined fish feed actively on nymphs, pupae, larvae, crustaceans and adult insects.

In lakes where forage fish are the salmons' main source of food, anglers usually concentrate their efforts immediately after ice-out along the shoreline shallows and around mouths of tributary streams where schools of spawning smelt tend to congregate.

Both cast and trolled floating or slow-sinking fly lines are preferred for this aspect of landlocked salmon fishing. Salmon streamer flies are almost always tied to resemble smelt or some other forage fish. Effective streamer fly patterns for landlocked salmon angling include: Black Ghost, Colonel Bates, Edson Dark Tiger, Gray Ghost, Nine-Three and Supervisor.

Dry flies, nymphs and wet flies suggesting the predominant hatches of the moment frequently prove effective when the salmon are feeding on aquatic insects.

Brook Trout

Few can deny the compelling, almost mystical beauty of that truly native American game fish the brook trout (*Salvelinus fontinalis*). Brookies, as they're commonly called, are regally decked out in bronze and green; iridescent blue, yellow and rose; speckled profusely with blue-ringed yellow and red spots. Their lower fins are colored hot orange and edged with black and white stripes along their anterior surfaces (Fig. 24).

Truly "wild" strains of brook trout are gradually disappearing from the North American scene, mostly because of their inability to cope with human encroachments on their watersheds. However, hatchery-spawned brookies are stocked in most of the United States and Canadian provinces. These fish provide some excellent fly fishing opportunities in several regions.

Brook trout are fall spawners that usually travel up inlet streams to complete their life cycles. They are also capable of successful spawning along the shoals of lakes. This natural ability of the brook trout to successfully perpetuate its race under a broad range of spawning conditions sometimes results in certain lakes becoming overpopulated with stunted, under-sized fish.

A brookie has a voluminous appetite and a short, powerfully efficient digestive tract. Lake-bred fish feed on a wide assortment of bottom-inhabiting creatures like mollusks, crustaceans and insect

Fig. 24. *This lunker brook trout succumbed to the seductive wriggle of a leechlike streamer fly.*

nymphs, as well as leeches, small fish and small terrestrial animals. The fact that brook trout are usually insatiable gluttons makes them reasonably vulnerable to the offerings of competent fly fishermen. However, brookies have moody, temperamental dispositions which make fly fishing for them not only interesting, but, sometimes, downright frustrating!

Usually the most productive way to fly fish for brook trout in early season is with the numerous, effective streamer fly patterns that represent forage fishes. The most effective retrieve under these conditions is usually fast and erratic . . . imparted in such a way as to make the fly appear to be a small fish trying to escape the trout.

Some of the most killing streamer fly patterns for brookie fishing in lakes are the Yellow and White Bucktail; Mickey Finn Bucktail; Nine-Three; Gray Ghost; Colonel Bates and Black Leech streamers.

As the lake waters warm in the spring and aquatic life becomes more active, brook trout vary their diet of fish with large helpings of mollusks, snails, scuds, leeches and nymphs. When heavy insect hatches are in progress brookies sometimes feed at the surface on adult insects and hatching nymphs. Some of the most telling nymph flies for luring brook trout near the lake bottom are the Gray Hackle; Henry's Lake Shrimp; the author's olive brown leech; Black Hackle; Heather Nymph; O'Gara Shrimp; Trueblood Otter Nymph; Leech Streamer and Dragon Fly Nymph. Dressings for all of these flies, as well as those listed for the other game fish considered here, are described in detail in the final chapter.

Browns in Lakes: A Different Sort of Challenge

Although the brown trout (*Salmo trutta*) is most commonly associated with classic eastern, midwestern and western trout streams, this popular European import with a penchant for surface feeding binges is no less eagerly looked upon as fair game by fly fishermen on numerous lakes and reservoirs.

The range of this wary, red and brown spotted battler has expanded to all but those states where the water temperatures are too high for even his remarkable tolerances. Brown trout are found in lakes and streams in virtually every region of the United States, as well as in South America, New Zealand, the British Isles, Europe, Canada and Tasmania.

Like brook trout, browns are fall spawners. Large, individual brown trout tend to be extremely nocturnal in their habits and feed almost exclusively on other fish. A fly fisherman with his heart set on catching a trophy-sized brown trout would do well to do most of his fishing with large streamer flies either very early in the morning or at night. However, there are notable occasions on which brown trout roam about near the lakes' surfaces, delicately sucking in adult midges and mayflies.

As a fighting fish the brown trout is tough and tenacious like a brookie, but, unlike the brook trout, will frequently jump clear out of the water in its efforts to escape the sting of a barbed hook.

Although the method may not appeal to totally stream-oriented brown trout buffs, trolling large streamer flies is probably the most reliable way to fish for large brown trout in lakes.

Virtually any streamer or bucktail fly suggesting a small fish may excite a hungry brown trout at one time or another. Some of the most consistently successful patterns are the Black Ghost; Atom Bomb; Gray Ghost; Marabou Perch; Marabou Muddler and Spuddler Minnow. In some lakes streamers like the Little Rainbow, Little Brookie and Little Brown Trout prove useful. One of the most deadly of all brown trout streamers, the Whitlock's Sculpin, is so complicated to tie that most amateur tiers won't attempt to dress it, but the authentic dressing is included in this book because of the pattern's effectiveness.

When conditions are right, nymphs and dry flies will hook their fair share of lake-inhabiting brown trout (Fig. 25). Virtually any patterns of nymphs, wet or dry flies suggesting a lake's predominant insects will catch brown trout provided the angler continually keeps in mind the ingrained wariness and keen eyesight of these fish.

Rainbows: Tops on Flies

Originally native only to rivers on our Pacific coast and Asian shores, rainbow trout (*Salmo gairdnerii; Salmo irideus; Salmo Kamloops*) have been introduced gradually into lakes, streams and rivers the world over. Today, these spectacular, dazzling fighters with the blush of carmine on their sides have found landlocked homes in the U.S.A., Canada, New Zealand, Europe, South America and Hawaii (Fig. 26).

Fig. 25. *A Spuddler Minnow streamer was the attraction that brought this 26-inch brown trout to the line.*

Fig. 26. *Daybreak fishing with size 12 Blue Quill dry flies helped catch these lake-bred rainbow trout.*

Rainbow trout usually spawn about April in temperate zone lakes, although the reproductive act can commence anytime between February and June, depending on the region, the strain of rainbow trout and water temperature. In flowage lakes with suitable inlet streams natural spawning can be performed quite successfully. But rainbow eggs require considerable agitation after fertilization and as a result, their spawning efforts in seepage lakes are mostly in vain. Good fishing for rainbows in seepage waters depends on periodic plants of either fingerling or legal-sized fish.

Rainbows consume the same basic food items as brookies and browns in lakes—nymphs, mollusks, crustaceans and small fish. The Kamloops strain of rainbow trout is a voracious fish-eater when forage fish inhabit the same water. In North Idaho and Canada the kokanee salmon, a nonmigratory sockeye salmon of fresh water, forms the primary food in the Kamloops' diet.

Long one of the most popular lake-inhabiting game fish with fly fishermen, rainbows enjoy rapid growth in rich waters, afford reasonably good eating and are usually willing to accept artificial flies.

Some of the most effective wet flies and nymphs for rainbow trout fishing are the Royal Coachman Bucktail, Gray Hackle, Black Hackle, O'Gara Shrimp, Little Rainbow Streamer, Yellow and White Bucktail, Heather Nymph, Black Midge Nymph, Grizzly King and Beaverpelt Nymph. Frequently useful dry flies are the Royal Coachman, Black Drake, Adams, R. B. Fox, Blue Dun, March Brown, Brown Midge, Black Ant and Tom Thumb.

Gentlemen Trout

Cutthroat trout range from the Dakotas to the Pacific Ocean and from the southern coast of Alaska to northern New Mexico. An honest-to-gosh North American "native" to the tip of his black-spotted tail, the cutthroat trout (*Salmo clarkii*) as a species is so riddled with subspecies, strains and cross-bred hybrids that sometimes it's hard to judge if a particular fish you've caught is a cutthroat or a rainbow, or, if a cutthroat, which kind. Even the telltale crimson markings on the skin of the lower jaw fail to make identification a positive matter.

Cutthroat trout spawn in the spring. Some strains, like the cutts found between the eastern slopes of the Cascades and the western

Fig. 27. *Cutthroat trout afford superlative action with the dry fly.*

side of the Rockies, are among the most avid surface feeding game fish in the world. Nicknamed the "red belly" by local anglers, because of broad swaths of pink or crimson on the lower sides of mature fish, this delightful trout is especially noted for its frequent midday feeding splurges during periods of maximum insect activity (Fig. 27).

The deep-bodied hybrid cutthroat-rainbows found in food-rich lakes like Henry's Lake, Idaho, and the west arm of Kootenay Lake, B.C., are especially prone to feeding on nymphs and shrimps, while the tackle-busting strain of cutthroat found in Pyramid and Walker lakes, Nevada, feeds mostly on other fishes.

Although few fly patterns suitable for brook trout, rainbow and brown trout won't attract cutthroats, it should be noted here that the more insectivorous cutthroat tend to be more gullible at times than their finned brethren. Four dry fly patterns will suffice in most regions: Royal Coachman Bucktail, Renegade, Mosquito and Adams. A few Gray and Black Hackles, Heather Nymphs, Black Ants and Dragon Fly Nymphs will catch cutthroats in most situations when the cutts are nymphing.

Dolly Varden

Regardless of one's opinion of the dolly varden as either a sporting fish or fierce predator of other fishes, the fact remains he is a significant and important game fish in many western waters from Montana to Alaska (Fig. 28). In Montana the local anglers refer to the dolly varden as a "bull" trout, which in this writer's opinion is no worse a malapropism than calling a female steelhead a "hen."

The dolly varden (*Salvelinus malma spectabilis*) is one of the most controversial of all the trouts and chars inhabiting North American waters. As fighting fish, these piscivorous, fall-spawning chars are quite unspectacular at the end of a line and very easy to catch from streams because of their tendency to school. In lakes, dolly varden lie at depths that discourage fly fishing most of the time. But they can be caught on streamer flies very early in the spring and late in the fall when they move into the shallows.

As a table fish the dolly varden is unsurpassed. Its delicate flavored pink meat is a succulent gustatory delight.

Fig. 28. *Dolly Varden may lack the spectacular fighting ability of other species of salmonids, but they more than make up for it at the table.*

Lake Trout

Lake trout (*Cristimover namaycush*), sometimes called "gray trout" or "mackinaw trout," are the largest of the chars and usually found in the deepest parts of deep, clear lakes—sometimes at depths approaching 200 feet! (Fig. 29).

Lake trout can be enticed with feathered offerings either early in the spring, immediately after ice-out, or late in the fall when they're over shallow shoals and shoreline ledges. The species has been introduced over most of the western United States and will be found from there all the way to Alaska in the north and east into Canada's vast, northern wilderness.

Trophy specimens of lake trout can be expected to put on a prolonged tug of war on light tackle, but for the most part these fish are quite unspectacular fighters.

Although they can occasionally be induced to take dry flies, lake trout more frequently are caught on six-inch long streamer flies representing forage fish.

Fig. 29. *Lake trout like this 12-pounder can be caught on large streamer flies near the surfaces of some lakes right after ice-out and again late in the fall.*

Fig. 30. *Smallmouth bass offer excellent game for the fly fishermen who seek them out in rocky lakes and streams. Their largemouth brethren provide top action on surface artificials.*

Bass Offer Superb Action

Largemouth and smallmouth bass, both sporty members of the sunfish family, may be North American natives, but today their ranges extend from coast to coast in the U.S. and Canada, into the Hawaiian islands, and onto the European and African continents.

Smallmouth bass (*Micropterus dolomieui*) inhabit colder, clearer waters than their largemouth kin and are found primarily in cold, rocky lakes and fast-flowing streams and rivers (Fig. 30).

Largemouth bass (*Micropterus salmoides*) are capable of surviving in waters up to 90° F. They are excellent fish for stocking in farm ponds and provide exciting fly fishing opportunities in most of the southern states as well as in numerous northern lakes and impoundments.

Both large and smallmouth bass respond enthusiastically to virtually any type of artificial fly, from tiny size 16 dry flies to bulky, wind-resistant size 3/0 creations fashioned out of deer body hair.

Bass spawn in the spring when the water temperature approaches 55° F. Bass feeding habits are highly omnivorous. They'll willingly gobble up insects, minnows, crustaceans, mollusks, leeches, waterworms, mice, frogs, bats and ducklings. Although early morning and late evening usually are the best times of day to cast surface artificials for these wary fish, bass can sometimes be caught on sunken flies in midday near deep weed beds, submerged rocky cliffs and lily pad areas.

Fig. 31. *Fly fishing for crappies can provide fast action. Some of the best locations in large reservoirs are partially submerged brush and willows (see lower left corner).*

First Rate Fly Fishing Fun

Take an insatiable appetite, squeeze it between a big mouth and a submoronic intellect, soak in lake water—and, you have a crappie!

There are two species of crappies in North America: black crappies (*Pomoxis nigromaculatus*) and white crappies (*Pomoxis annularis*). Regardless of which type of crappie is abundant in your area, these flaky-meated panfish can provide you with great fun on a fly rod. Black crappies are most often encountered in the northern states, white crappies in southern waters.

Crappies spawn sometime between January and July, depending on the region. The spawning fish school in large numbers in shallow bays (Fig. 31). Because of their predatory tendencies, crappies are most readily taken on small streamer and bucktail flies resembling forage fish like shiners and immature perch.

Some of the most effective crappie flies are simple bucktails with silver tinsel bodies and either yellow and white or red and white wings. Sophistication is totally unnecessary in crappie flies.

During the late spring and summer months, when the crappies feed on hatching insects periodically, small cork-bodied popper bugs on size 8 or 10 hooks are extremely effective. Some anglers prefer cork-bodied bugs to conventional dry flies for crappie fishing. The cork bugs don't waterlog like regular trout flies.

Surface feeding crappies usually take artificial flies quite eagerly, but when a crappie sucks in a fly beneath the surface, recognizing the take is sometimes next to impossible. It's not unusual for neophyte fly fishermen to have difficulty recognizing the very gentle way a crappie practically inhales a wet fly or streamer. It takes experience before most fly fishermen learn to set the hook at the slightest hint of the line tightening or the feeling that the fly is dragging across a soft weed. The slightest resistence encountered while retrieving a wet fly can signal the delicate take of a crappie.

Bluegills

Bluegills (*Lepomis macrochirus*), or "bream" as they're often called in the South, are the most popular and widely distributed of all the sunfishes. Bluegills are especially appropriate game for fly fishermen. Their diets consist mostly of insects, nymphs, larvae and small crustaceans. Pound for pound, bluegills put up as good a scrap

Fig. 32. *Pound for pound, bluegill is one of the scrappiest fish on light fly fishing tackle.*

on ultralight tackle as any of the more spectacular, large game fish (Fig. 32).

In the northern regions of the U.S. the bluegill is a spring spawning species. But, in the relatively warmer waters of the Deep South, these scrappy little panfish are known to spawn as often as three times a year!

Bluegills can be caught on numerous types of small flies, but for the most fun, fish for them with tiny cork poppers or dry flies when they surface feed on warm spring and summer evenings. When bluegill are spawning, small wet flies like the Gray Hackle, peacock body, are sometimes very effective.

If You Fish for Meat

Of all the lake fish that respond to artificial flies, the yellow perch (*Pesca flavescens*) is one of the easiest to catch and tastiest on the table. Perch range from northern Alberta to the Carolinas and from Nova Scotia to the Pacific Ocean in North America.

Yellow perch spawn very early in the new year. They usually begin to gather in large schools over suitable shoals or in spawning inlets shortly before or after ice-out. I know of some lakes where the perch school as early as December.

Adult perch are extremely carnivorous fish. They'll eat almost any kind of small fish, insect nymph or crustacean. Small wet flies, nymphs and streamers are consistent perch killers. Two of the best patterns are the Gray Hackle, peacock body (tied with a scarlet tail) in sizes 10 and 12; and the Edson Dark Tiger bucktail, dressed on a size 10 or 12, 3XL hook. A rather slow, jerky, erratic retrieve usually produces the most strikes from perch.

If the lake isn't ice-covered at the time, the fastest fly fishing for perch can be had when the fish are on their spawning beds. But generally speaking, perch can be caught on wet flies virtually anytime of the year. They almost always seem to be hungry!

More Fly Fishermen Should Try Walleyes

The walleye (*Stizostedion vitreum vitreum*), sometimes referred to as the walleyed pike or pike perch, is not a true pike. Instead, the walleye is the largest of the freshwater perches.

Fig. 33. *Walleye and northern pike are prevalent in many out-of-the-way northern lakes.*

Mr. Walleye's range extends from Lake Athabasca through Hudson Bay drainages in the North, and south through the Atlantic states to North Carolina. The species is abundant in the Great Lakes region, in the Mississippi river valley to the Tennessee River in the East, and to northern Arkansas in the West. Isolated populations of walleyes are found in some of the western states as well.

Walleyes spawn in the early spring, occasionally before the spring ice-out. They spawn over rocky or gravelly lake bottoms. A good time to take them on a fly rod is when they're spawning in shallow water. At other times walleyes lurk near rocky, wave-swept shores near points of land, or in bays with sand or gravel bottoms.

Streamer flies are usually the most useful flies for walleye angling. These voracious predators feed mostly on smaller fishes (Fig. 33). Although they can be caught at any time of the day, walleyes tend to move into the shallows in early evening to feed on minnows. Some of the best opportunities to catch walleyes on flies occur after dark.

Fig. 34. *A high, saillike dorsal fin characterizes the male arctic grayling (above). The female (below) has a smaller, rounder dorsal.*

Arctic Grayling

Relatively few American fly fishermen have caught arctic grayling. Their native habitat is mostly so remote from population centers that the cost of fishing for grayling discourages anglers of modest means. Those who have cast dry flies and nymphs to these delightful game fish, both the arctic version and its Montana counterpart, consider the grayling a very sporty fish indeed.

Arctic grayling are splendidly garbed and readily identified by their high, saillike dorsal fins (Fig. 34). The grayling's range courses across most of the northernmost regions of Canada, from British Columbia to Manitoba. They are also abundant in the state of Alaska. Stateside, grayling are found only in some of the waters in the states of Montana and Wyoming.

Grayling (*Thymallus arcticus*) are generally small fish that average a pound or less in weight. However, some lakes and streams contain "trophy class" grayling from two to five pounds in weight. These unusual fish vary considerably in color, depending on the time of year and where you find them. Some emanate a purplish caste, while others exhibit a silvery, bronze or overall bluish patina.

The grayling's back is usually dark, bluish gray or black and its sides spotted with bluish black or purple towards the head. In addition to these spots, there are two dark spots on the skin of the grayling's lower jaw, in about the same position as the crimson markings appear on the lower jaws of most cutthroat trout strains.

A grayling's prominent dorsal fin, which somewhat resembles the dorsal of a sail fish, is usually dark in color and covered with incredibly beautiful flame blue or purple spots. Occasionally, the spots on the dorsal fin are edged in red. Montana grayling have red or purple dorsal markings edged in green, but are considered by most experts to be part and parcel the same fish as the arctic grayling.

Grayling spawn in April or May in their extreme southerly range and as late as June in the far North of Alaska and Canada. Most of the spawning takes place in streams tributary to lakes; however, some spawning activity on the part of grayling has been observed in shallow bays of lakes over sand or gravel bottoms.

Some literature on the subject of grayling (there really hasn't been much written about them) suggests they feed predominantly on tiny insects, because of supposedly small mouths. That isn't true. A friend and I once caught and released some 400 arctic grayling in a week's time—mostly on sizes 12, 10 and 8 dry flies. The grayling would readily take smaller flies, to be sure, but the largest fish we caught on that trip (those from two to four pounds) mostly succumbed to the enticement of size 10 Grizzly Wulff and caddis flies. The predominant insect hatches in that particular area consisted mostly of fairly large mayflies and caddis. No doubt in regions where no large insects exist grayling are forced to feed mostly on smaller insects like midges and mosquitoes.

Effective fly patterns for grayling fishing will vary, depending on the natural foods available to them in each specific area. Excellent patterns for dry fly fishing are the Grizzly Wulff, Royal Wulff, Light Cahill and Black Gnat in sizes 14 through 8.

Some anglers believe that arctic grayling are frequently too easy to catch to be sporty quarry. It's true that these high-jumping beauties can be very cooperative during massive insect hatches and mating flights. But, although small grayling are frequently overenthusiastic about taking artificial flies, the large, hard-fleshed trophy grayling can be quite difficult to interest with feathered steel. British Columbia fisheries biologist David Hurn aptly stated the case for grayling when he said: "Grayling are a near perfect quarry for fly fishermen. They do precisely what they're supposed to do—if you do what you're supposed to do!"

Trophy-class arctic grayling favor lake and stream locations where they don't have to work hard to gather food. I've observed they especially favor under-cut banks, the edges of eddies, deep pools at the toes of rapids flowing into lakes and shoal areas adjacent to lake outlets (Fig. 35).

On the other hand, small-sized grayling are apt to be hooked virtually anywhere in a lake or stream, including areas adjacent to very fast current. A really large arctic grayling rarely takes up a feeding station right in fast water. In lakes the grayling are mostly found in relatively shallow water where there is an abundance of aquatic insect life.

In the relatively slow-moving types of water they most assuredly prefer, large grayling have adequate time to closely examine any artificials that float over them. One gorgeous, blue bronze beauty I caught refused nearly a dozen apparently perfect drifts of my dry fly before finally engulfing the artificial.

Fig. 35. *This arctic grayling high jumper pounced on a size 12 Grizzly Wulff dry fly.*

Pike—Explosive Action!

Northern pike (*Esox lucius*) are extremely predatory game fish normally found in the relatively shallow parts of lakes and rivers above the 40th Parallel. Pike are so fiercely aggressive towards other fish and small terrestrial animals they're often called the "tigers" of the North Country.

Pike are probably the easiest of the large, North American game fish to coax to streamer flies and surface bugs—yet, few anglers try for them with fly fishing methods. Many northern pike enthusiasts figure the only way to catch pike is with plugs or wobbling spoons. Having fished for pike extensively both ways, I can say it's been my experience that pike in shallow water come as readily to flies as they do to plugs and lures (Fig. 36). Fly fishing for pike is superb sport —full of explosive surprises and action! More people should try it.

Northern pike spawn in the shallow portions of lakes immediately after the ice breaks up in the spring. Virtually any large, colorful streamer fly or bass bug will instigate a savage attack by a pike at

Fig. 36. Northern pike like the fish at right come readily to streamer flies and surface bugs in early spring. Below, this 15-pounder followed the fly almost to the boat before grabbing it.

Fig. 37. The author examines one of the 6-inch-long, red and white streamer flies he prefers for pike fishing.

that time of the year. Some of the most effective pike streamers are tied about six inches long in yellow and white, yellow and red, orange and red, and black and green combinations (Fig. 37). The pattern doesn't seem to be very important as long as the fly is fished slowly.

Because of the pike's razor sharp teeth, it's essential to use a two- or three-foot long "shock tippet" of heavy 40- to 60-pound test hard nylon monofilament at the business end of your regular leader. Long leaders aren't necessary for northern pike fly fishing. Tie them out of "hard" nylon monofilament, tapering them to 15-pound test at the point, then attach the shock tippet (Fig. 38). The entire pike leader is less than nine feet long. Even when you're using heavy shock tippet you'll occasionally suffer the disappointment of losing a hefty pike when a tooth slices the heavy shock tippet on the strike. Fly fishing for northern pike is a very sporting proposition. The odds are better than 50-50 in favor of really big pike because of those incredibly sharp teeth and their effect on monofilament leaders!

Four Big Fly Fishing Secrets

In order to fish effectively with flies on a consistent basis it's necessary to catalyze one's knowledge of lakes and angling theories with attitudes which sharpen powers of concentration and observation, and stimulate a willingness to experiment and persist. Persistence, experimentation, concentration and observation are the true "secrets" of successful fly fishing.

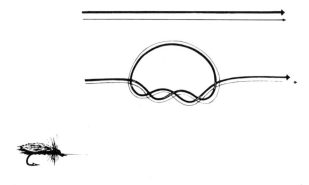

Fig. 38. *The knot for affixing the shock tippet to the leader is fairly simple to tie.*

Fig. 39. *Heather Roskelley displays some nice crappies caught on a day day when persistence paid off.*

I recall a day when persistence meant the difference between getting "skunked" or catching a sack full of crappies! A friend and I were fishing a large reservoir where the previous weekend we'd experienced considerable success catching crappies. We caught crappies on practically every cast the preceding Saturday along a shore lined with heavy growths of partially submerged willows. On this trip, however, the "hot spot" was totally devoid of crappies. We fished an area of over 500 acres without locating a single crappie! After three hours of steady casting we possessed three small perch.

It was quite clear the schools of crappies had deserted the willow-lined bay for parts unknown. The arm of the reservoir was several miles long. Locating the departed crappies seemed hopeless. We had a nearly full gas tank, so we decided to undertake a thorough search of the entire arm of the lake. We cast and retrieved our wet flies off likely looking points of land; in deep water, shallow water and water of medium depth; along other willow-lined shores and even in the flow of an inlet stream, hop-scotching along the better part of four miles of shoreline. Persistence paid off two hours later when we located a tremendous school of crappies feeding actively near a willow-fringed point of land. Hooking fish on virtually every cast with our bucktail flies, my companion and I caught all the plump ¾-pound crappies we wanted in less than an hour (Fig. 39).

Willingness to continue fishing, even under certain kinds of adverse weather conditions, has its payoff, too! One day Tommy Stouffer and I were fly fishing on a small rainbow trout lake when an incredibly violent rainstorm moved into the area. Strangely enough, the storm contained no lightning and only minimal wind so we remained on the lake clad in rain suits. The rainstorm was so pelting and dense we could scarcely see more than 50 yards in any direction. All the other anglers fishing the lake ran for shore. Within moments of the start of the rain the rainbow trout went on what remains to this day the most fantastic surface and near-surface feeding binge I've ever experienced. It seemed that every trout in the lake was trying its darnest to get caught. We hooked and released so many trout from nine inches to four pounds during the course of the next two hours that our arms ached. When the rain finally subsided the trout stopped feeding.

3

Tackle

Before delving into the specific techniques of fishing lakes with flies a brief discussion of fishing tackle might be helpful.

Rods

Effective lake fishing with flies is sometimes a highly demanding exercise for the fly caster. Casts of 60 to 80 feet are often absolutely essential to achieve the desired results. Because of this fact, an eight- to nine-foot fly rod with a smooth, full length flex and a medium to fast action is ideal for most lake situations. Such a rod has the potential to deliver long, straight casts under windy conditions—a common problem of the lake fisherman.

Anglers with more than the usual casting skill may prefer fly rods with actions termed "slow" or "parabolic." However, many of these relatively slim-butted, progressively tapered fly rods require a finely tuned casting hand in order to fully realize their remarkable potential for accuracy and distance.

One's casting ability isn't the only factor affecting the choice of fly rods for lake fishing. Rods used primarily for fishing deeply sub-

merged nymphs and streamer flies on sinking lines must have sufficient overall power from butt to tip to quickly straighten the "belly"
of the line following a strike. On the other hand, the relatively powerful rod used for deep line work is not the best choice for the nerve-
racking delicacy required to fish dry flies and nymphs on extremely
fine leader tippets. A near-surface nymphing and dry fly rod should
have casting power, to be sure, but also should possess enough delicacy in the tip action to allow for setting the hook with fine tippet
material.

Few if any glass or bamboo fly rods are ideally adaptable to every
conceivable lake fishing situation. Most experienced lake fly fishermen employ no less than two, and usually three rods—a reasonably
powerful eight to nine footer for sinking line work, a seven- to eight-
foot dry fly-action rod for floating lines and a nine- to nine-and-a-
half-foot bass-action rod for casting large, wind-resistant streamers
and bass bugs.

Five- to six-foot long ultralight fly rods are delightful stream fishing
instruments. But, unless you happen to be a superlative caster, I can't
honestly recommend them for fishing lakes in windy situations. It is
difficult enough for two accomplished fly casters, each exercising a
maximum amount of courtesy, to fly fish a lake effectively from the
same boat with relatively long rods. When the wind is up, short fly
rods unduly complicate the job. Personally, I find little amusement in
having fly hooks surgically removed from various portions of my
anatomy! Short rods multiply that risk in the wind.

Fly rods ideally suited to lake fishing are marketed by Berkley &
Company, Cortland Line Company, Daisy-Heddon, Daiwa, Eddie
Bauer Expedition Outfitters, Fenwick (Sevenstrand Tackle Manufac-
turing Company), Garcia Corp., Orvis, Phillipson, Russ Peak, Scientific Anglers Inc., South Bend Tackle Company, R. L. Winston Rods
and Wright & McGill Company to name just a few. Other fine fly
rods are manufactured in England by Hardy Bros. and in France by
Pezon et Michel. Several major rod manufacturers offer rods with
good actions for lake fishing at very reasonable prices. Then there
are the numerous fiber glass and bamboo rod blanks available to
anglers who want to mount their own rods. Some of the best blanks
are sold under the Grizzly-Fenwick and Orvis labels. Fig. 40 on
page 66 contains detailed recommendations for rod lengths and
actions for various types of lake fly fishing.

Fig. 40   ROD-LENGTH RECOMMENDATIONS

Type of Fishing	Species	Rod Length	Rod Action	Backing Line	Leader Length	Tippet Side	Lines
Streamer flies	panfish	7½-8 ft.	slow	none	7½ ft.	4 lb. *.0085	Weight forward II or III sinking
Streamer flies	trout salmon	8-9½ ft.	fast to med.	50-150 yds.	7½-11 ft.	4-10 lb. .008-.012	Weight forward II or III sinking
Streamer flies	bass walleye n. pike	8½-9½ ft.	slow to med.	50 yds.	6-9 ft.	8-20 lb. plus shock tippet for pike	Weight forward II or III sinking
Deep nymphs	panfish	7½-8 ft.	med. to fast	none	7½ ft.	4 lb. .008	Weight forward II or III sinking
Deep nymphs	trout grayling	8-9 ft.	med. to fast	50-100 yds. large fish	7½-15 ft	3-8 lb. .007-.011	
Deep nymphs	bass	8-9 ft.	med. to fast	50 yds.	6-9 ft.	6-10 lb. .010	
Shallow nymphs	panfish	7½-8 ft.	slow to med.	none	7½ ft	2-4 lb. .0055-.008	Weight forward I sinking, or sink tip, or floating
Shallow nymphs	trout grayling	7½-9 ft.	slow to med.	50-100 yds.	7½-15 ft.	2-8 lb. .0055-.011	Weight forward I sinking, or sink tip, or floating
Shallow nymphs	bass	8-9 ft.	slow to med.	50 yds.	7½-9 ft.	6-10 lb. .010	Weight forward I sinking, or sink tip, or floating
Dry flies	panfish	7½-8 ft.	slow to fast	none	7½ ft.	4 lb. .008	floating
Dry flies	trout grayling	7½-9 ft.	slow to fast	50-100 yds.	7½-15 ft.	1-6 lb. .004-.010	floating
Dry flies (bugs)	bass n. pike	9-9½ ft.	slow to med.	50 yds.	6-9 ft.	8-20 lb. plus shock tippet for pike .015	

*All tippet sizes are approximate. Those listed here are based on Pezon at Michel "Kroic" leader material. Some materials, like Garcia's Platyl, are smaller diameter per pound test. Others are larger. Author prefers "Kroic" and improved "Stren" because of their knot strength.

Reels

Reels for fly fishing lakes should be large enough to hold sufficient backing line for the species of game fish you seek and be so constructed as to provide many years of trouble-free service. Some of the best reels for lake fishing are the Daisy-Heddon "lightweight" series, the Orvis "Battenkill" in standard and lightweight models, the Garcia "Beaudex" and "Pridex," Pfleuger "Medalist" and "Su-

Fig. 41. *Recommended types of single-action fly reels for lake fishing: top, left to right, Orvis Battenkill and Daiwa 252; bottom, left to right, South Bend Finalist and Scientific Anglers "System" Reel.*

preme" fly reels, the Scientific Anglers, Inc. "System" reels, and several models with the Daiwa label. The discontinued custom-made Thompson fly reels and the Hardy "Princess," "Zenith," "St. George," "St. John," and "Perfect" reels are all well suited to lake fishing.

Single action fly reels like those illustrated in Fig. 41 are the most useful type for lake fishing. I don't recommend automatic fly reels for any species of game fish requiring the use of large amounts of backing line. Fig. 42 on page 68 recommends reel drum sizes and backing line requirements for the various North American lake gamefish species.

One of the secrets of handling large, fast-swimming fish successfully on light tackle is to allow the fish to run when it wants to. How tight or loose you adjust the drag on the fly reel can make the difference between landing a big fish and completely bungling the job. For fast-moving fish, like rainbow trout and landlocked salmon, set the drag adjustment just tight enough to prevent the reel from overrunning when a big one takes off. Once you've adjusted the drag to the proper tension, *leave it alone*! Indiscriminate fiddling around with the drag adjustment can result in it being inadvertently set too tight to pay out line rapidly. For most fishing situations the drag should be set quite light so that line pays out freely when the fish runs. Once the fish stops running away from you it's safe to apply all the pres-

Fig. 42   Recommended Reel-Drum Sizes
For Lake Fly Fishing

SPECIES	DRUM SIZE	BACKING LINE
Panfish	3½" or smaller	not required
Walleye	3½" or smaller	seldom needed
Trout (7"-14")	3½" or smaller	not needed
Trout (15"-4 lb.)	3½" or larger	50 yds.
Trout (4 lb. & up)	3½" or larger	up to 200 yds.
Bass	3½" or larger	rarely needed but 50 yds. recommended
Pike & Muskie	3¾" or larger	50 to 100 yds.
Landlocked Salmon	3½" or larger	100 to 200 yds.

Fig. 43   Recommended Types of Fly Lines
for Lake Fly Fishing

Fishing Type	Taper	Sinking Fly Line Types						Floating Fly Lines		
		I	II	III	ST	WH	LH	Reg.	BT	SWT
Dry Flies	WF,DT							X		
Bass Bugs	WF								X	X
Streamers (shallow)	WF	X	X		X			X	X	X
Streamers (deep)	WF		X	X			X			
Nymphs (shallow)	WF	X			X			X		
Nymphs (deep)	WF		X	X		X	X			

KEY: WF — Weight-forward
DT — Double-tapered
I — AMFTMA designated for "slow-sinking" line
II — AMFTMA designated for "fast-sinking" line
III — AMFTMA designated for "extra-fast-sinking" line
ST — Sinking Tip (front six or eight feet)
WH — Wet-Head (front 30 feet sinks)
LH — Lead-Head (a line into which two feet or so of lead-core line
         has been spliced, usually at the tip end)
BT — Bug-Taper
SWT — Salt-Water Taper

sure your leader tippet will withstand. But, when the fish makes the reel "sing," never try to stop the run completely unless the fish is headed into brush or some other type of underwater entanglement.

Fly Lines

Modern sinking fly lines (Fig. 43) designed specifically to sink flies fast and deep, are responsible for much of the modern revolution in lake fly fishing methods.

Sinking fly lines are constructed in several ways. Some are made with a thin-diameter lead core woven inside a braided line that's finished with a plastic coating. In my opinion, the best line of this type was first marketed by the B. F. Gladding Company under the trade name "Aquasink."

Other great sinking fly lines are constructed of a solid, braided dacron core over which a special finish is applied, ground and polished to the desired taper. The best lines of this type are made by Scientific Anglers, Inc., under the trade name "Wet Cel," by the Cortland Line Company under the trade names "'333" and "444" sinking lines, and by the Newton Line Company. There are other brands of sinking fly lines available, some good, some not so effective, but the Scientific Anglers, Cortland and Newton lines are the best I've tried to date, not only for their sinking qualities but also for their castability.

As is true in the case of floating fly lines, modern sinking lines come in a variety of tapers: level, double-tapered, weight-forward and shooting head. Level fly lines are useful for trolling on lakes, but that's all. The long casts frequently necessary to fish sinking fly lines effectively are most easily accomplished with weight-forward tapered lines. Near-surface nymphing and dry fly fishing are likewise most effectively performed with weight-forward tapered floating, slow-sinking and sink-tip lines on lakes. Weight-forward fly lines require fewer false casts and perform better into the wind than the double-tapered lines preferred by most experienced stream fishermen. Double tapers are useful on lakes only when the water is glassy smooth and an extremely delicate delivery of the fly is required.

Although tremendously long casts can be made with sinking shooting-head lines, their use on lakes presents a number of incontestable drawbacks. For one thing, the monofilament shooting line commonly used with these popular lines designed for river fishing tends to tangle when used in a boat. And then there's that helpless situation that comes about when one's 30-foot shooting head becomes snagged on some lake bottom obstruction in water over 30 feet deep! In the opinion of most experienced lake fly fishermen who've tried shooting heads, their disadvantages outweigh their occasional usefulness in most situations. Shooting-head fly lines perform best in the water for which they were designed—large, fast-flowing streams and rivers.

In addition to being available in various tapers, sinking lines are also made in models that sink at different speeds: slow-sinking, fast-sinking and extra fast-sinking (Fig. 43). Slow-sinking fly lines are designated by the roman numeral "I" as a prefix to the standard AFTMA weight designations, i.e. I-WF-7-S, which in this case specifies a slow-sinking, weight-forward fly line weighing between 177 and

193 grains in the forward 30 feet. Roman numeral "II" denotes a fast-sinking line, and extra fast-sinking models are specified by Roman numeral "III" as a suffix to the weight-type-style code (Fig. 44).

For normal deep fly fishing in lakes you'll need two forward-taper sinking fly lines, one a type II fast-sinker and the other a type III extra fast line to efficiently probe depths in excess of 15 feet.

For fishing at depths of less than six feet, the slow-sinking and sink-tip styles of lines are most useful. Sink-tip lines consist of a few feet of sinking line at the tip with the remainder of the line a floater.

It probably wouldn't make any difference if sinking lines were colored purple with orange spots, but for dry fly fishing line color is extremely important. Since the following remarks on this subject may be in serious conflict with some firmly entrenched opinions on fly line color, let me preface them by saying my conclusions are drawn from over 30 years of fly fishing on lakes (and streams) totaling thousands of hours of practical, on-the-water experience.

Now, for the bombshell!

Fluorescent red and orange demonstration-casting floating fly lines are my A-Number One choice for dry fly fishing on lakes. These colorful lines were originally produced for exhibition casting by professionals. They appear so gaudy in the air and on the water one might be tempted to conclude they would scare the daylights out of any game fish. But they don't! Fluorescent fly lines don't frighten the fish any more than soft green or mahogany colored lines, even

Fig. 44-B AFTMA Fly Line Weights

WEIGHT CODE	WEIGHT	ALLOWABLE TOLERANCES
4	120 gr.	114-126 gr.
5	140 gr.	134-146 gr.
6	160 gr.	152-168 gr.
7	185 gr.	177-193 gr.
8	210 gr.	202-218 gr.
9	240 gr.	230-250 gr.
10	280 gr.	270-290 gr.
11	330 gr.	318-342 gr.

Note: Line weights 1, 2, 3 and 12 have been omitted from this chart because they have little or no application to lake fishing situations.

Fig. 44. *Here are two popular makes of packaged lines available to fishermen throughout the country*

in extremely clear, shallow water. And, the fluorescent fly lines are extremely visible to the angler on overcast days and during the early morning and late evening hours when neutral colored lines are practically invisible. Both Cortland Line Company and Scientific Anglers, Inc. manufacture fluorescent floating lines.

Next to the fluorescent colors, my second choice is a white or ivory floating fly line. They're only slightly less visible in dim light than fluorescent lines. Light green and amber floating lines rank third on my list of color preferences. They're plenty visible in strong light and when the water's relatively unruffled by the wind. The same thing goes for lines colored mahogany and dark green.

Color is relatively unimportant when it comes to sinking fly lines. The hook is set by feel in that phase of the sport, rather than by sight as in dry fly fishing.

Leaders

Long leaders are generally preferred by experienced lake fishing buffs, at least when it comes to angling for leader-shy trout. Most experienced lake fly fishermen tie or purchase trout leaders in lengths varying from nine to 15 feet. Leaders for crappies, pike, bass and panfish needn't exceed seven and one-half feet because none of those species is exceptionally leader-shy.

In general, it pays to select leaders with the smallest diameter tippets that will safely handle the fish you seek and still promote proper turnover of the fly at the end of the cast. Follow the recommendations on tippet size in Fig. 40 and you won't go far astray. Keep in mind that highly air-resistant flies do not handle well on excessively fine tippets. Conversely, it isn't recommended that a fellow try to affix tiny size 20 to 26 midge flies to the same size tippets he might use when fishing streamer flies. Even if he could pass the heavier leader through the eyes of the small hook (which in some cases you can't), the knot would end up nearly as large as the flies themselves.

If you think stream fish are fussy about floating leader tippets, just wait until you start fishing dry flies and nymphs on the glassy, unruffled surface of a clear lake! Sometimes it's necessary to sink the tippet in order to elicit any strikes at all from wary trout and salmon, especially when fishing tiny dry flies and those wispy, hard-to-sink creations tied to suggest hatching midge pupae.

Both the diameter and the flexibility of the leader material used for lake fishing can be important. Hard nylon butt sections promote better leader turnover than extremely limp nylon. But, hard nylon is difficult to straighten in cold weather. Most lake fishermen I know are showing increasing interest in untempered leader materials like "Maxima" and "Kroic," both European imports. These leader materials possess excellent knot strength and straighten easily. They are stiff enough in larger diameters to promote good leader turnover, yet limp enough in the smaller diameters used as tippets to enhance the action imparted to nymphs and streamer flies.

Individual casting style and ability strongly affects a fellow's preference in the matter of leader "taper." If you are a complete beginner at the sport of fly fishing, let me suggest you purchase tailor-made leaders at the start. Most of the ready-made leaders have been designed by experienced fly fishermen and will perform very well. On the other hand, if you are already an experienced fly caster, you no doubt have settled on leader designs that best suit your casting style. If that's the case, you'll be much happier, and fish better, by adapting the leaders you already use to the lake fishing situation.

4

How To Fish Streamer Flies

Recall from Chapter 1 our discussion of the tendency of most large, freshwater game fish to feed on other fish. It is precisely because of the predatory nature of many gamefish species that streamer flies suggesting small fish are so effective. Common forage fish like smelt, gamefish fingerlings and the numerous species of minnows may be found in virtually any lake capable of sustaining aquatic life (Fig. 13). An abundance of forage fish in a lake containing predatory game fish impacts heavily on fishing methods.

For example, American smelt are an extremely important forage fish for landlocked salmon and lake trout in the northeastern United States. They move in schools into the tributary streams and along the lake shore shallows soon after ice-out in the spring. Trout and salmon follow the schooled smelts and feed heavily upon them. Fly fishermen can capitalize on the phenomenon by casting and trolling streamer flies resembling the smelts.

Out West in the mountain states, lake fishermen take advantage of the brown trout's fall spawning habit by concentrating their efforts with large streamer flies adjacent to known spawning streams and shoals. And, of course, the gluttonous brookie is especially susceptible to the enticement of a fish dinner throughout the entire season. The shallow water spawning habits of numerous fish-eating sport fish like crappies, walleyes, pike, muskies and trout put them well within reach of fake minnows during their various spawning seasons, as described in Chapter I, as well as periodically throughout the remainder of the year.

Developing Effective Retrieves

A lake fisherman's efforts to effectively manipulate his flies beneath the surface are relatively complex. In a stream the current frequently imparts enough action to a submerged fly to provoke a fish into striking. In lakes the fly fisherman himself must make his artificials behave like living aquatic creatures. He controls the behavior of his flies both by means of retrieve and fly tying technique.

Streamer flies can be dressed in various ways to influence their behavior in the water. Some are tied to "swim" smoothly when trolled or retrieved (Fig. 45). Others are dressed with splayed feather wings or fluffy marabou feathers to give the appearance of breathing and darting when twitched through the depths. Some streamer flies are attempts to represent the actual colors and shapes of specific species of baitfish. Others are conglomerates of colors known to attract certain game fishes.

Think Like a Fish

Retrieve is the lake fisherman's most important control over the behavior of his flies beneath the surface. Strike-provoking retrieves are the product of converting impressions of how minnows and nymphs swim, dart and crawl into coordinated physical manipulations. In a sense, to emulate the movements of underwater creatures with artificials one must learn to "think" like fish and nymphs.

A good way to learn the principles of thinking like a forage fish is to spend an afternoon at an aquarium. Notice how each species of fish, from the smallest to the largest, has a particular way of propelling itself through the water, feeding and escaping from the threat of predation by other fish. Before long you'll realize that some fish,

Fig. 45. *Types of streamers.*

like catfish, are extremely lazy creatures. They'll spend long periods resting near the bottom and, when they feed, they'll eat mostly bottom inhabiting organisms. You'll be fascinated by the shy little sculpin minnows' ability to conceal themselves under stones. Both the slimy and mottled sculpins serve as food for lake trout, brown trout, brookies and landlocked salmon. If you're able to visit some game department fish hatchery which raises several species of trout and panfish you'll immediately detect behavioral differences between the young game fish, some of which will help you develop retrieves for imitative streamer flies. Then, as you extend your aquatic observations to lakes you'll be treated to the sights of both poised and prowling trout and salmon, the frantic darting of schooled minnows being ravaged by large game fish, the rapierlike attack of a pike, and a thousand other insights into fish behavior. With these personal observations well in mind it will then be time for you to start fishing streamer flies.

Many effective streamer fly retrieves are based on a technique called "stripping." First, a cast of the required length is made and the fly allowed to sink to the depth you want to fish. Then, lengths of line (from a couple of inches to a foot or more) are recovered with your retrieve hand in pulling motions that "strip" the line through the guides on your fly rod (Fig. 46). The time interval between the pulls, the speed with which they're imparted and the length of each pull can be applied in countless variations to suggest the movements of most types of forage fish. That's why it's so important to observe the movements of live fish *before* attempting to suggest their movements via retrieve. Personal observations are absolutely essential to developing effective retrieves, although occasionally we chance on killing methods quite by accident.

Take as an example a retrieve that's sometimes effective when

Fig. 46. *Hand positions during the "stripping" retrieve.*

brook trout are feeding on small fish. The method was first described
to me by my friend Mike Runje. I named it the "Runje Twitch!"

One day I drove into Mike's service station for a lube job on my
pickup truck. As Mike serviced the vehicle we began to discuss
fishing, not at all unnatural since we both belong to the same fly
fishing club.

Runje remarked how the previous day he'd enjoyed excellent
action on a pond containing two- to six-pound brookies. Naturally,
I was all ears!

"You know," he said, demonstrating with a grease-stained red
bandana, "we couldn't get a bump until we retrieved our bucktails
very rapidly, like this. We'd make a few long, fast strips, allow the
fly to rest motionless in the water for a long moment, then give it a
twitch with the rod tip! About the same time we'd twitch the fly a
big ole brookie would pile into it! Wow! Some fun!"

Now, it just so happened that Roskelley and I had a trip planned
to the same lake for the very next day. Early in the morning we

arrived at the fabulous brookie pond, the exact location of which is a carefully guarded secret by the several thousand local anglers who are aware of its potential!

"You say Mike did good here last Tuesday?" asked Roskelley as we bounced along the rough dirt track leading to the water's edge.

"Yup," I grunted in my most convincing, deadpan expression. I'd conceived of a nonmalicious though somewhat fiendish plan to needle my pal and said "Mike said he used the fast strip," failing to mention the little twitch that produced the strikes.

The brook trout were unusually phlegmatic that day. Fast, medium and slow retrieves alike were met with total indifference by the lake's overfed brookies.

"Wouldn't you know it!" exclaimed my pal after an hour of unproductive casting and retrieving. "Those darn brook trout would pick today to be persnickety!"

Our lack of success was puzzling. Everything seemed right for catching out-sized brook trout—rising barometer, dark phase of the moon, stiff gusts of wind lashing the surface of the 33-acre pond, overcast skies. "What more could a brookie want to stimulate his appetite," I thought.

I waited until Roskelley was deeply absorbed in a subtle retrieve —and tried the Runje Twitch!

Whammo! My rod tip was yanked violently down into the water as a slab-sided three-pounder clobbered my Colonel Bates Streamer less than 15 feet from the boat.

"Well!" exclaimed Ross in a relieved tone. "That's encouraging!" He eyed my fly as I removed the hook from the fish, continuing his close surveillance of my every move through two casts and retrieves. Naturally, I didn't impart the twitch when he was watching.

Finally, convinced he could copy my retrieve to the last detail, he made a cast and turned away when I was halfway through a retrieve. Immediately, I imparted three very fast strips to the line, paused and gave the fly a twitch.

Bang! A much heavier fish than the first socked my streamer so hard the four-pound-test tippet parted.

"Fast strip again?" choked Roskelley, his face a kaleidoscope of mixed emotions!

"Sure," I lied blandly. "You know me!"

"That's what I mean," he chuckled and made another cast.

Ross stopped eyeing me suspiciously several minutes later. I imparted the Runje Twitch once again and a five-pound brookie socked the fly and wallowed to the surface. This was the opportunity to drive home the needle.

"What's-a-matter?" I asked as condescendingly as possible. "Can't you get the hang of it? Lake's alive with fish. See. I'm playing another big one!"

If my pal had been a beginner instead of one of the finest lake anglers in the country the rattled expression would have been pitiable. But, to a fishing pal of over 15 years it was hilarious! I couldn't maintain the poker-faced front any longer and began to bray, as Ross put it, "like an utter jackass!" I laughed so hard that tears flooded my eyes, causing me to bungle the landing of the five pounder.

Having had a little joke at his expense I proceeded to share the "Runje Twitch" with my friend. I made another cast, stripped in rapidly four or five times, paused and twitched my streamer fly. Another five pounder came thrashing to the surface.

"You bum!" chuckled Roskelley. He made a couple of casts and landed two huge brookies using the same retrieve.

Although it is impossible and could be misleading to set down hard and fast rules concerning retrieve techniques, each gamefish species exhibits a certain more or less general affinity to either fast, medium or slow recoveries.

As the preceding anecdote suggests, brook trout are frequently most susceptible to very fast-moving streamer flies, except when the water temperature is extremely cold or when they're foraging for slow-moving aquatic insects or snails to the exclusion of baitfish. The landlocked salmon is another fish that more often than not ends up swimming in a dutch oven because of his excessive enthusiasm over fast-moving streamers. Rainbow and brown trout react positively towards streamer flies retrieved over a wide range of speeds. Northern pike, walleyes and crappies on the other hand respond most avidly to very slowly retrieved flies as do largemouth and smallmouth bass.

Water Temperature Influences Retrieve Speed

Water temperature is an additional factor strongly influencing how fast to retrieve streamer flies. In general, most North American game fish respond best to the faster retrieves when the water temperature ranges somewhere between 50 and 65° F. When the water temperature is 45° F or less the odds are great that slower retrieves will produce more strikes.

Try to relate retrieve speed both to water temperature and the behavioral peculiarities of the various species of game fish. For example, on most lakes containing rainbow trout it pays to fish streamer flies quite rapidly during the late spring, early summer and fall months. But, during the winter and early spring—when the water temperature runs between 34 and 45° F—you'll probably catch more fish if you retrieve your fake minnows very slowly, at least until you're convinced the slow retrieves are unproductive. I recall a frigid, early March day when I hooked and released several large trout from a reservoir by slowly inching a black streamer fly over gravel shoals. By the middle of the following April it was necessary to troll perchlike streamer flies very rapidly to induce strikes from the fish in that same body of water.

Another good example of the effectiveness of the slow retrieve took place on a nameless little pike lake. My companion was using size 2 gray and black deer hair bass bugs in his efforts to hook the hefty pike we'd located in a shallow bay. I was fishing with a surface line also. However, I selected a size 3/0 yellow and red feathered streamer for pike enticement. Both of us employed "dead slow" stripping retrieves, allowing our flies to remain motionless for as long as 20 seconds between the long, slow recoveries of the line. We caught pike until our casting arms ached! For nearly four hours we hooked and released pike on virtually every cast. By way of experimentation, each of us would periodically try a fast retrieve. None of the fast retrieves elicited strikes. As soon as we'd return to the slow recoveries of our lines, hefty pike from six to 16 pounds would sock our flies.

Walleyes are terrifically susceptible to the slowly retrieved streamer flies. I'll never forget the time at Jan Lake, Saskatchewan, when "Tony" Sturek of Oak Lawn, Ill., and I hove to in a broad shallow bay teeming with walleyes. Large numbers of tiny black midges were hatching at the surface. Sizable schools of forage fish were gobbling up the midges. And, walleyes from two to four pounds were feeding on the minnows.

Tony started fishing his favorite red and white Lazy Ike plug on a light spinning outfit. The walleyes would take occasional passes at the normally deadly plug, but on this occasion they were hitting short and Tony was missing the light strikes.

I tied a size 2 Light Tiger bucktail on my tippet for openers. Following my initial cast, I hadn't stripped in over three feet of line when a seven-pound pike nailed the fly. The pike's teeth made a shambles of the soft chenille body of the fly. I changed to a steelhead fly with a durable, lacquered tinsel body.

My first cast was met by a hungry three-pound walleye that soon ended up on the stringer. For the remainder of the afternoon Tony and I took turns using the fly rod. We each boated fine catches of walleyes and, in addition, caught ourselves several more pike—all of them on flies.

Bass also usually respond best to slowly retrieved streamer flies. When a foreign object like a fly lands in the water near a bass he'll usually swim off several feet, stop and eye that object with considerable suspicion. Bass are extremely wary, keen-eyed fish. The bass will usually watch the fly with diminishing concern until he's convinced it means him no harm. Then his gluttonous nature takes over. If, after several minutes, that feathered creation twitches and starts to slowly swim away like a minnow, it's a very unusual bass that will fail to try for an easy meal. Let your fly sink nearly to the lake bottom before starting your retrieve. The bass will usually hit before the fly has had a chance to move more than six feet—it he's going to hit at all.

Crappies also are especially susceptible to the spells cast by slowly wiggling feathers and bucktail. One day we located a large school of crappies near where a stream dumps into a large impoundment. We had bagged about two dozen of the tasty panfish when some friends appeared in a boat and began to cast their flies. Strangely, they couldn't seem to hook any crappies despite the fact they were using almost identical flies and sinking fly lines. Not wanting to see our friends go home fishless we observed their retrieve methods closely for a few minutes. They were employing fast stripping retrieves, so fast in fact that it's doubtful if the crappies could catch their racing feathers and steel! After convincing them to use dead-slow recoveries they soon began to connect with fish. They left for home with all the fish they could carry.

Trolling: Popular and Effective

Trolling is one of the most popular and effective ways to fish with streamer flies in lakes. The method is an especially efficient way to locate wandering schools of crappies and walleyes, as well as helpful in locating concentrations of game fish in totally unfamiliar water.

Three basic trolling methods are well adapted to streamer fly fishing: powered trolling, "mooching" and wind-drifting.

Powered trolling is generally the most effective trolling technique to employ when a steadily swimming, fast-moving streamer fly is indicated, as is often the case when landlocked salmon are feeding on schools of smelts. The basics of powered trolling are quite simple to master. Up to three lines can be effectively fished from most boats under power. In the case of large, outrigger craft, a fourth line is sometimes used, though not recommended. One of the best three-line trolling setups is to let out a short line directly astern so that the fly works in the wash of the motor. Twelve to 20 feet is usually enough for the short line. Run out the starboard line about 40 feet and the port-side line between 60 and 80 feet. That way there's less chance of the lines becoming fouled if two fish are hooked simultaneously.

Virtually every type of line in the fly caster's arsenal, as well as several other types, can be employed to troll streamer flies with motor-powered boats. There are many anglers who rarely fish with anything but streamers and wet flies towed along behind their boats on monofilament, lead-cored or metal trolling lines.

Actually, the rods and lines you select for trolling flies depend mostly on the species of fish you seek, how deep you intend to fish and whether or not you intend to do any casting. Conventional, star-drag trolling reels and light-action boat rods are good choices if you do not plan to cast. The better grades of freshwater trolling rods and reels are rarely as expensive as the best fly rods and reels.

A fellow could cope with virtually any streamer fly trolling situation in North America with two rods, three reels and three lines, none of them conventional fly fishing equipment. One could be a spinning rod rigged with a monofilament line testing 6 or 8 pounds. The other two outfits could be boat rods and reels, one rigged with a star-drag, level-wind reel loaded with lead-cored trolling line, the other a star-drag, free-spooling reel containing monel or braided steel line.

On the other hand, the fly fisherman could get by with two fly rods and five lines for his fly trolling vacation. Both the heavy-action bass rod and the eight- to nine-foot deep nymphing rod mentioned in Chapter II would serve nicely for the variety of conditions one might encounter across this country and Canada. One large-diameter fly reel with five extra spools would handle the required lines. These would include one spool filled with 6-pound monofilament and no fly line, a floating fly line, and slow, fast and extra-fast sinking fly lines.

Methodical combing of the water by following certain trolling patterns is the procedure used by most successful streamer fly trollers. The waters adjacent to rocky reefs, points of land, submerged cliffs and islands are methodically probed by maneuvering the boat through series of "figure-8," S-shaped and criss-cross trolling patterns (Fig. 52), varying the depth you fish and the speed you troll until game fish are located. Once you locate the fish it pays to troll back and forth through the productive area until you cease to get strikes. Fish are located by first "reading" the lake by means of the principles outlined in Chapter I, then caught by experimenting with trolling speed, depth and fly patterns. There's no complicated "mystique" to any kind of fishing with flies. Your success will be directly in proportion to how well you apply your knowledge of fish, fish habits, fish foods and lakes to each angling situation. Luck also enters the picture, probably more in trolling than in other forms of lake fly fishing. Most certainly, one should expect less success on unfamiliar waters than on lakes he fishes regularly. Try to remember that it's not at all uncommon to get "skunked" on your first trip to an unfamiliar lake. All of us periodically get our "noses wiped" by the fish—sometimes even on lakes with which we are intimately familiar. Fishing probably wouldn't be half the fun it is if we all caught lots of fish on every trip.

One of the most interesting afternoons of streamer fly fishing I can recall occurred when I was fishing for crappies in a very rocky, somewhat turbid lake of medium depth. The ice had gone out a few days earlier and the lake had turned over, giving the water a strange, creamy green tint. I had never fished the lake before, so I began to troll very slowly through areas that looked like they might hold crappies. I trolled with power, I wind-drifted, I mooched, trying nearly a dozen different streamer and nymph patterns. The crappies were simply not to be found! I figured I was about due for a "skunking!"

Deciding to call it quits, I trolled slowly back toward the rocky boat launching area near an earth-fill dam. As I approached the dam I noticed considerable fish activity along the rip-rap of the dam proper. The feeding fish looked suspiciously like rainbow trout. I cut off the motor and began to cast wet flies and streamers on a sinking fly line towards the fish, retrieving them back slowly with stripping and hand-twist retrieves. The rolling fish appeared to be feeding on smaller fish, possibly young perch or crappies. I whipped a size 10, 3XL Perch Fry bucktail to my tippet and made a few casts, again without a response.

Becoming more frustrated by the moment, I decided to troll several times through the area in which the fish were feeding, this time quite fast. Halfway through the first pass a 14-inch rainbow grabbed the perch imitation and thrashed to the surface! During the next hour I trolled a fast figure-8 pattern, thoroughly combing the area where I'd first spotted the feeding trout. That first fish contained several newly hatched fish fry. I changed to a size 14, 3XL streamer fly of similar color and proceeded to catch several fat rainbows, averaging a pound and a half apiece! As one of my chums might put it: "The green gods of food fortune were smiling that day!"

Mooching Is Deadly

Fly fishermen borrowed the term "mooching" from a bait fishing technique used by some Pacific Northwest salmon anglers. The method is well suited to fishing nymphs and streamer flies at depths up to 30 feet.

In order to mooch a streamer fly or nymph the angler works out 30 to 90 feet of fly line (fast-sinking, extra fast-sinking, slow-sinking, sink-tip or floating lines all can be used, depending on the depth you want to fish) behind the boat. The line is allowed to sink to the desired depth. The angler then rows the boat with oars at varying speeds, pausing at times to let the fly sink, speeding up on other occasions to suggest to the fish the fly is trying to escape (Fig. 47). Insofar as the fisher of streamer flies is concerned, the technique is especially well suited to angling for crappies, trout of most species,

Fig. 47. *Mooching is a technique that brings success to many, as above near the likely-looking brush pile.*

smallmouth bass, largemouth bass, muskies, walleyes and northern pike. Mooching is usually so productive a method that considerable numbers of lake fishermen fish no other way.

Exploration of unfamiliar lakes is one of the more valuable uses of the mooching technique. I have personally depended on the mooching of flies to quickly acquaint me with the "hot spots" in lakes from New Jersey to British Columbia, lakes containing four species of trouts and chars, the basses, pike, walleyes and panfish, including yellow perch.

The method is frequently deadly on bass waters during the late evening or early morning hours when the bass desert their midday cover and roam the shallows in search of forage fish.

Locating roving schools of game fish is another useful application of mooching. The technique pays off regularly when you're fishing for crappies in large, hard-to-read reservoirs. For example, take a more or less typical day on a lake known to harbor large schools of spawning crappies. Our knowledge of the habits of these fish tell us that, when they're spawning, the schooled crappies will be gathered in large numbers around creek mouths and in bays where the water is fairly shallow and the lake bottom is sandy or gravelly.

By first flying over the lake in a plane or by consulting depth charts of the lake or employing a sonar device, it's easy enough to pinpoint those areas most likely to contain spawning crappies. A very fast boat is useful for this type of fishing. You can run quickly from one likely location to the next, pausing to mooch streamer flies through the prospective crappie beds until you locate the fish. Once you locate the fish by mooching methods, then anchor and continue fishing by casting and retrieving.

Mooching is also highly productive when a fellow's trying to emulate certain slow-moving aquatic creatures, like crayfish and leeches, with streamer flies. My log books indicate dozens of occasions when the method was killing on brook trout ponds and lakes containing leeches, and on northern pike and walleye waters. By far one of the most exciting nights of rainbow fishing I've ever experienced occurred while mooching crayfishlike streamer flies adjacent to vertical rock cliffs on a 400-acre desert lake. Between 9:30 and 11:00 P.M. I hooked the rocks at the lake bottom some 50 times, ran into the cliffs proper over a dozen times, had my four-pound test leader parted thrice by heavy strikes and landed three rainbows that weighed a total of 10½ pounds! Not a bad catch for less than two hours of fishing in the dark.

Wind-drifting is the other trolling method for streamer flies that frequently produces action. It's accomplished by positioning the boat upwind of the lake area you want to fish, working out the desired amount of floating or sinking fly line, and allowing the breeze to push the boat along the trolling path (Fig. 48). Additional action is sometimes imparted to the fly by twitching the rod tip or stripping in line during the course of a wind-drift trolling pattern. The method is useful on the same broad variety of game fishes as mooching. It's especially helpful to wind-drift when you want to work a fly over spooky fish in very clear water, to suggest the strugglings of a crippled minnow near the surface or when slow-moving caddis pupae are rising to hatch. Wind-drifting is also an excellent way to fish flies representing hatching midge pupae on floating lines. Generally speaking, this technique is more frequently effective used in conjunction with nymph flies than with streamers. And, it's a deadly way to emulate the slowest movements of leeches with imitative feather-winged

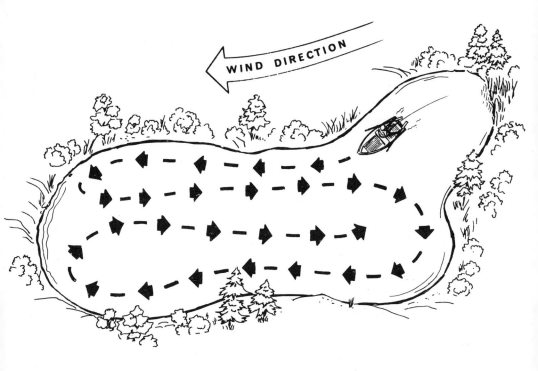

Fig. 48. *Here is a wind-drift trolling pattern in a 20-acre pond. Drift downwind, then "mooch" back and repeat.*

streamer patterns, as well as to swim minnow fakes through the shallows frequented by walleyes during their nocturnal feeding forays.

One of the most useful applications of the wind-drift troll is when you are seeking out concentrations of spawning northern pike shortly after ice-out along the shoreline shallows, and in the late fall when pike are frequently found lying in relatively deep weed beds. Pike seem to respond most avidly to extremely slow retrieves. Accomplished on a light breeze, pushing the boat along more or less parallel to the shoreline, wind-drifting is one of the best ways to locate concentrations of pike. Once you locate a fish or two, then row back to the area where you hooked them, anchor and cast.

5

How to Fish Deeply Sunken Nymphs

Deep-water angling methods employing fast- and extra fast-sinking fly lines are generally the most logical choices when observations fail to disclose gamefish feeding activity near or at the surface of a lake. Nymph and streamer flies suggesting the underwater creatures that comprise about 80 percent of most game fishes' diets are our "meat and potato" offerings, while nymphs fished near the surface and dry flies tend to put the "frosting" on the fly fishing cake.

An Intriguing Challenge

In some ways the fishing of nymphs at or near the lake bottom is the most demanding test of a lake fisherman's skill and judgement. He is in fact fishing "blind," relying entirely on his knowledge of limnology, entomology and ecology to locate hungry fish, and on his past successes to suggest effective means of enticing them to the fly. Another factor enters the picture, too. It's a relatively rare day on a stream of moderate size when you're faced with the absolute necessity of making numerous casts in excess of 50 feet. Actually, it's preferable when stream fishing to wade to where you can make even shorter casts than 50 feet. The shorter casts allow you to achieve the pinpoint accuracy needed to effectively probe small pockets, eddies, slicks, hard-to-reach runs beneath bushes and next to under-cut banks. Shorter casts also allow the stream fishermen to more adequately compensate for line drag by means of the mending technique with a floating fly line. And, it is unquestionably easier to hook fish at short range than far away.

Long Retrieves Often Needed

Lakes present complex retrieve problems. When fishing blind in a lake it is of paramount importance to keep in mind that the greater the distance you retrieve your nymph through potential gamefish feeding areas, the more likely it is that fish will see that fly and the better your chances of provoking strikes and hooking fish.

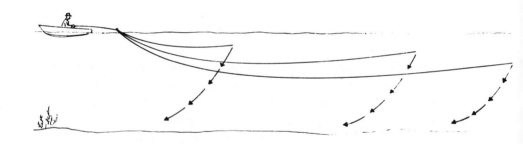

Fig. 49.   *Retrieves can be effective whether long or short, but the long ones offer the best opportunities.*

Assume you are anchored near a weed bed where fish are known to feed on some bottom-inhabiting creatures, like snails, at a depth of 20 feet. If the farthest you can cast is 20 feet then your sinking line will carry the fly down to where, when you begin your retrieve, the fly will return in a nearly direct vertical path to your rod tip (Fig. 49). With a 20-foot cast over 20 feet of water your fly cannot possibly probe the weed bed's potential fish-holding area in an effective manner. By using a little "guestimated" trigonometry to account for the belly in the sinking line and the angle at which it lies in relation to the lake bottom and you at the surface, you can calculate that a cast of 65 feet or more will be required to achieve 30 feet of really effective retrieve in 20 feet of water!

How many fly fishermen in your circle of angling acquaintances can cast a measured 65 feet? How many can knock out 80 feet of line? Probably not more than a half dozen anglers in your entire region can cast 80 feet or more consistently and accurately. Yet, in order to become a consistently successful deep-line fly fisherman it's frequently necessary to make those long, long casts with weight-forward sinking lines.

If you happen to be a relatively short caster at this stage of your development into a fly fisher of lakes there are a number of ways to improve your distance casting skill. There are several useful tips on improving casting in Chapter 8, But the best way to learn how to make long casts is to take a series of lessons from a professional caster. His trained eye and helpful coaching can guide you along the path to casting skill with a minimum of time and effort wasted. Another means of developing casting ability is to join one of the numerous casting clubs throughout the country where adequate practice pools and competent amateur (and sometimes professional) instruction is available. Of course, if your fishing buddy is an outstanding distance caster there's the tried and true method of swallowing your pride and asking him for assistance. Whatever means you employ to improve casting will certainly pay dividends out on the lake.

Long, effective retrieves are tremendously important in many deep-water angling situations. Take as an example a trip three of us took to a 16-acre, spring-fed pond. This particular pond is relatively deep and bowl-shaped, affording no extreme shallow areas. The water depth averages 15 feet and runs to 30 feet. The bottom of the pond is covered with a sparse carpet of chara weeds over a mud base.

One of the fellows in the fishing party was a delightful companion, but nonetheless incapable of making long casts. His longest cast wouldn't exceed 30 feet, unfortunately. Fishing was slow that day, but the two of us who could knock out 70-foot casts and retrieve our nymphs close to the weeds at the lake bottom managed to catch fish. The short caster didn't get a single strike! He simply couldn't make long, effective retrieves with his short casts.

Putting in the "Wiggle"

Throughout this book I have and will continue to refer to "effective" retrieves and fishing methods. As it applies to deep nymph fishing, an effective retrieve can be defined as one during which a type of "action" is imparted to the fly by the angler that convinces the fish the artificial is a living, edible aquatic creature.

Effective retrieves are developed by first observing the size, shapes, colors and consistencies of reallife nymphs and crustaceans, then suggesting their forms in our creations at the fly tying vise, and finally, by imparting to those creations movements that suggest life. Two of the most consistently effective ways to manipulate deeply sunken nymph flies are the "stripping" method described in the chapter on streamer fly fishing and the "hand-twist" retrieve popularized by the late Ray Bergman.

The hand-twist is probably the most deadly of the two techniques in relatively cold waters or when one wishes to emulate the slow clambering of mayfly, damselfly and dragonfly nymphs and crayfish, the numerous antics of scuds and the wriggling of midge larvae. It is also an excellent way to suggest the crawling and gliding of snails and cased caddis larvae. Faster hand-twist retrieves are often used to imitate the upward swimming of damselfly nymphs, the short, darting movements of dragonfly nymphs and the undulating movements of leeches.

Hand-twist retrieves can be imparted in an almost infinite variety of rates and frequencies, from the dead-slow crawl effective in winter's chill waters to the fast, jerky recoveries often deadly during periods of maximum aquatic insect activity.

To recover line with the hand-twist, grasp the fly line between the thumb and index finger of your retrieve hand (Fig. 50). If you're a right-handed caster use your left hand to impart the retrieve. If you're left-handed then use your right hand for retrieving. Next, pull in anywhere from one to three inches of line towards your palm. Now, rotate your wrist and recover more line with the remaining three digits of your retrieve hand. Repeat this procedure varying the rate and frequency of the twists until you're ready to lift the line from the water to make a new cast.

The stripping method described in Chapter 4. (Fig. 46), is usually the most effective when imparted at relatively fast tempo to suggest

Fig. 50. *Hand and finger positions during "hand-twist" retrieve sequence.*

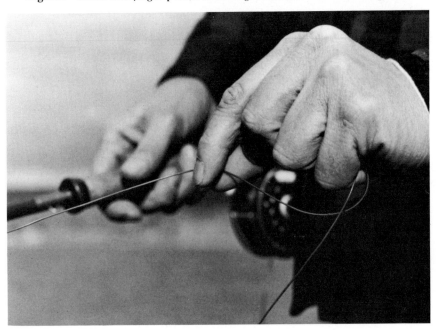

the darting of dragonfly nymphs, and fast swimming and darting of minnows. At slower tempos stripping is a good way to emulate swimming leeches, slowly rising caddis pupae and damselfly nymphs, and scuds and snails that have been rooted loose from the lake bottom by feeding fish.

Often, one can combine the hand-twist and stripping retrieves to good effect. There is a 33-acre pond not far from my home where I learned a valuable lesson about the importance of experimenting with retrieves. At that time in the late 1950s I was struggling to discover new methods that would catch fish when the normally effective stripping retrieve failed. For many months I had been studying retrieve methods described in the numerous angling tomes on my library shelves. Lake fishing literature is relatively scarce. Most of the books contained information predominantly aimed at stream fishermen. Then, I finally chanced on the hand-twist method described by Ray Bergman in his classic volume, *Trout*. I began to experiment at various lakes with the method and soon discovered that although hand-twisting was occasionally productive, it didn't catch fish with the same degree of consistency as stripping. I didn't entirely write off the method, but wanted to be more adequately convinced of its effectiveness over a wide range of angling situations.

So it was one sunny afternoon on that gorgeous little lake teeming with 12 to 20-inch rainbow trout that my angling education was fingered by fate. I'd fished without a strike for an hour and a half using every variation of the hand-twist and stripping methods I could imagine. Then, during one very fast stripping retrieve, I saw a large trout follow my Heather Nymph and suddenly veer away as the fly approached the shoreline where I stood. The water was clear, but the low afternoon sun caused a harsh reflection that hampered the view. I put on a pair of polaroid sunglasses to improve my ability to observe the fly as it approached the shallows. During the next three fast retrieves rainbow trout followed the fly, turning away at the last possible moment near shore. As my fly approached the shore during the next retrieve I observed a good-sized trout following it. Something prompted me to stop the retrieve momentarily, then impart a half dozen quick, short hand-twists. Bang! The trout nailed my nymph with a rush! From then on, the fishing that afternoon was almost too easy. Within a half-hour I'd hooked several husky fish, releasing all but two fat 15 inchers for the pan. I lost one "gran-daddy" trout that would have gone five pounds!

That revealing experience adjusted my whole approach to the matter of retrieve. I began to reason that the more or less mechanical patterns of retrieve I'd been employing were based more on instinct than on my first-hand observations of the subtle variations of loco-motion used by live aquatic insects. I began a systematic study of how each of the creatures fish feed upon actually behaved in the water. The results changed my method drastically. I began to "think" more and more like a nymph or minnow trying to escape a predator as I imparted movements to my artificials, at the same time trying to visualize how a hungry game fish might respond to them. By more closely approximating with retrieve the movements of aquatic crea-tures—by being increasingly less concerned with fly patterns and more intent on achieving long, effective retrieves—I was able to increase to a marked degree my success when fishing with deeply sunken nymphs. Now, when I arrive at an unfamiliar lake I don't even bother to string up a fly rod until two preliminaries have been accomplished—taking the water temperature to determine the prob-able degree of insect and fish activity, and sampling the aquatic life at the lake bottom to get an idea of what flies and retrieves offer the best chances of success. By using this method, fishing with deeply submerged flies ceases to be purely a matter of blind luck. Coupled with a knowledge of where game fish are likely to be found the method affords every possible opportunity for success!

There's more to successful deep nymph fishing than merely locat-ing fish and developing retrieves that interest them. For example, how do you present a fly at precisely the same depth, cast after cast, after you've coaxed that first fish of the day into striking? Three methods come to mind immediately: by-guess-and-by-gosh, the actual timing of the artificial's rate of descent with a watch, and a useful, old-time technique with a space-age name—the "count-down."

"Count-Down" to the Fish

Guessing how far your fly has settled into the water is okay if you're fishing in relatively shallow water, say, up to about six feet. But, a fellow's assessment of elapsed time tends to be erroneous over periods in excess of ten or 15 seconds. It's obvious that the most accurate way to determine how deeply a sinking line and fly have sunk is to time their descent with a watch. But, in some instances that method is impractical—especially if you happen to have left your wrist watch on the night stand or dressing table. A less troublesome way to accomplish the objective of an accurately timed sink of fly and line is to count mentally as they descend into the depths, "One-one thousand, two-one thousand, three-one thousand, etc." (Fig. 51). On the other hand, if you are getting your strikes at considerable depth requiring a sink of perhaps a minute or two, then very possibly you'll decide to time by means of a watch. All this depends pretty much on how intently you want to concentrate on the count. Regardless of your counting method, the important thing is to fish each cast at the depth you received the initial strikes from the fish. Fishing at a certain depth can make all the difference in the fish catching department.

I'll never forget the day we discovered a school of crappies at a depth measured by 17 counts! The crappies were so concentrated at that depth that on several casts I allowed my fly to sink to the seventeenth count, set the hook instinctively and hooked a crappie!

Where you anchor your boat in relation to channels between weed beds, reefs, shoals, submerged islands and other underwater obstructions is also important when fishing with deeply submerged nymphs. A long, narrow channel between weed beds is usually best fished by anchoring the boat bow and stern, cross-ways to one end of the channel, then casting parallel to it so that your flies can be retrieved down its length. Shoals are quite interesting in that game fish will sometimes lie in the deep water along their outer perimeters during midday hours, then, during insect hatching periods (which can occur virtually anytime during the day or night) move into the shallows to feed. When the fish are obviously lying in the deep water, anchor right on top of the shoal and cast your nymphs on an extra fast- or fast-sinking line, retrieving them up along the ascending slopes of the submerged shoal or reef. Once the insects begin to hatch and the fish move to the shallows to feed on them, then reanchor in deep water and cast a slow-sinking, sink-tip or floating line over the shallows. The same procedure is applicable to fishing the shoreline "food shelf" of a lake where it drops in relatively abrupt fashion into deep water.

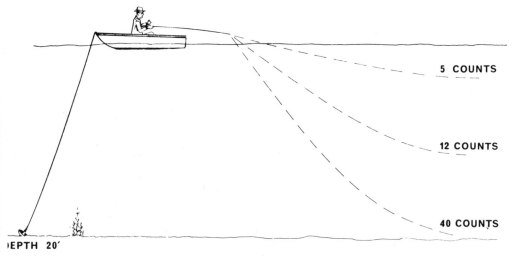

5 COUNTS

12 COUNTS

40 COUNTS

ⅠEPTH 20′

Fig. 51. *Diagram of what counts generally amount to with extra-fast sinking line.*

Exploring Unknown Waters

Fly casting purists may be slightly repelled by the prospects of trolling with flies. But the fact remains that trolling nymphs is one of the best ways to explore unfamiliar lakes and locate fish in waters you know only slightly. Sometimes trolling is the most effective way to fish a deeply submerged nymph. For example, there's a truly delightful 100-acre oval of water where a trolled nymph produced fantastic action. The bottom of the lake is more or less bowl-shaped, averaging about 20 feet deep. The trout there grow up to 18 pounds!

I fished this hidden trout haven for the first time with a friend from California by the name of Grant Markman. The sun was playing peekaboo behind threatening storm clouds when we dumped his car-top boat into the lake about noon. The water was slick, gray, dead looking. Few insects were about and no fish could be observed feeding near the surface. Grant said that he'd caught fish virtually everywhere in the lake, mostly by trolling a small, silver wobbling spoon. Using an outboard motor for propulsion we began to troll around the lake some 50 yards from the shoreline. Grant started out with his favorite wobbling spoon, while I tried a black-bodied Carey Special fly on a fast-sinking line for openers.

We trolled very slowly for nearly an hour without a bump. Then, I spotted some floating snail shells.

"I believe I'll change to a fly resembling a snail," I grinned. "I'd lay odds the fish are right down on the bottom amongst the weeds, rooting out snails and gobbling them up as they float towards the surface!"

A large, deep-bodied rainbow swirled nearby. I plucked a size 2 brownish gray glob of spun fur from my fly box. The fly is called a Beaverpelt nymph, for very apparent reasons, and was devised by biologist Don Earnest, a dedicated wet fly fisherman. Don's one of the several angler-scientists who were so helpful to me in reducing a vast accumulation of scientific facts and figures into reasonably understandable lay terminology for the first chapter of this book.

Shortly after I tied the out-sized furry concoction to my tippet the first fish socked it. The rainbow hit at the end of a broad turn as we swung parallel to a submerged weed bed in about 15 feet of water. By the time I realized what had happened, the rainbow was three feet out of the water! Then, the fish took off on a bullish, reel-screeching run for the opposite shore of the lake. Some ten minutes later 26 inches of exhausted trout flopped in the net.

Markman squinted throughtfully as I removed my nymph from the trout's lip.

"Might have been a mistake," he chuckled. I dressed the fish immediately, wanting to know what it had been feeding on, if anything. A half-dozen snails and four long, gray black leeches tumbled out of the trout's stomach. Grant didn't need further convincing. He pounced immediately on one of my Beaverpelt nymphs and tied it to his tippet. Within two hours we'd caught two 20-inch-plus fish apiece and lost several others.

Mooching, as we pointed out in the chapter on streamer fly fishing, is especially useful for exploring unfamiliar lakes, locating roving schools of fish and emulating the movements of slow-moving aquatic creatures. When exercised in conjunction with streamer flies it will be found highly productive on virtually every freshwater gamefish species. Those fish most attracted to mooched artificials representing aquatic insect nymphs, crustaceans and leeches include rainbow, cutthroat and brown trout, smallmouth and largemouth bass, crappies, perch, sunfishes and northern pike.

The basic method employed to mooch deeply sunken nymph flies is the same as is used to mooch-troll streamer flies. Sinking line is cast or otherwise worked out to the desired distance. The line is allowed to sink to the depth you want to troll. Then the boat is moved along slowly by taking an occasional dip on the oars. The water is combed by maneuvering the boat parallel to shore, or in criss-cross, lazy-S, figure-8 or circular patterns, whichever scheme most adequately adapts to the area being fished (Fig. 52). Periodically during a mooch

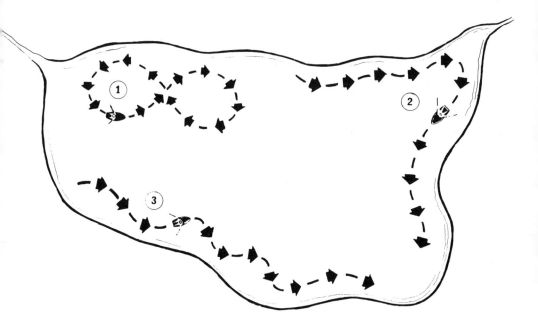

Fig. 52. *Some basic trolling patterns for fly fishing: (1) Figure 8, frequently used to explore tops of submerged reefs, weed beds, etc.; (2) S Pattern, used to explore points of land, inlets, outlets; (3) Multi-directional pattern, used to probe rocky shorelines, shoals, and extensive weedy areas.*

troll the really experienced lake angler will stop rowing and impart variations on the hand-twist and stripping retrieves hopefully to provoke a strike from any fish that may be following his flies out of curiosity. This little variation on the mooched fly is frequently killing when the fish aren't taking hard enough to hook themselves.

Wind-drift trolling, although best adapted to the use of floating or sink-tip fly lines, does have a place in the deep-nympher's bag of tricks. As in the case of mooching nymph flies, wind-drifting is especially useful when you want to emulate the underwater movements of slow-moving creatures like leeches, snails and caddis pupae. The rudiments of wind-drifting were discussed in the chapter on fishing with streamer flies and needn't be repeated here, since it is a method used only when the strength of the breeze and conformation of the lake make it the best choice (Fig. 48).

6

Near-Surface
Nymph Fishing

Many of the popular North American game fishes, most notably
the basses, trouts and pan fishes, feed actively on hatching aquatic
insects, both as the nymphs and pupae are rising or crawling to the
surface and as they struggle to free themselves of their casings. These
electrifying moments occur frequently in the spring and fall when
aquatic insect activity hits periodic peaks.

The "when," "how" and "what with" of effectively imitating the
prehatching and hatching efforts of insects presents a considerable
challenge to a fellow's knowledge and adaptability as a fly fisherman.
Let's start by examining some of the indicators of when one should
fish artificial nymphs close to the surface.

Visible fish activity near the surface, coincident with insect hatching, is one relatively reliable indicator that near-surface nymph fishing might be successful. Swirling game fish, rises that merely bulge the
water's surface, the faint V-shaped wakes caused by fishes' dorsal
fins as they cruise along looking for food, "tailing" rises—all are
reasonably certain signs of nymphing fish. Rises that break the sur-

face film, dimpling rises and those in which the fish make audible sucking sounds usually, though not always, indicate fish feeding on adult insects. Often the fish will be taking in nymphs and adult insects simultaneously, as is frequently the case during massive hatches of midges, caddis flies and mayflies. A little experimenting with both artificial nymphs and dry flies will usually indicate which method is most productive at a given moment.

More difficult to assess are those occasions when game fish are actually feeding quite near the surface without disturbing its calm, as in the case of game fish gorging on slowly rising caddis pupae at depths of one to six feet. In this type of situation knowledge of a lake's ecology and the seasonal behavior of the game fish and their food organisms strongly influence your relative success at the game of educated guesswork called "nymphing." For example, if you're fishing a lake in the early spring, well before the time mayfly, dragonfly and damselfly hatches can be expected, and observe flurries of fish activity near the surface, it is logical to assume that the fish may be feeding on midges or forage fish. If that lake contains no forage fish, as is the case in "rehabilitated" waters where the scrap fish and forage fish have been chemically eradicated, then the list of possible explanations is drastically narrowed. And, if you make a few casts using a nymph resembling a midge pupa and hook some fish, you can reasonably assume your hunch was correct. An immediate check of a fish's stomach contents should confirm or deny your conclusion. In addition to midges it is possible that the fish, in this case, might also be feeding on water-fleas, shrimps, snails, water beetles and other types of insect nymphs.

Back to Retrieve

Retrieves based on the movements of living aquatic creatures influence our success at near-surface nymphing in the same ways as they affect our deep-water efforts with nymphs and streamer flies. One learns to impart effective retrieves to near-surface artificials by closely observing the naturals. By way of review, let's reexamine the hatching of certain important nymphs and pupae.

Even many nonfishermen are aware that midges are relatively tiny insects as adults and are frequently confused with mosquitoes because of similarities in appearance. Game fish feed on midges in both underwater and adult forms. The young midges, called larvae, are cylindrical in shape. The larvae are usually red, white or green in color. Midge larvae, which look rather like small worms, are eaten in extravagant quantities by the fish at the lake bottom, where they're grubbed out of the mud, debris or decaying organic matter.

Midges hatch after their larval worms pupate and reorganize their parts into adult insect form. At hatching time, as the pupal skin of some midge species splits, the adult inside lashes its abdomen to assist itself in wriggling out of the shuck. Other midge species hatch in relative quietude.

Because midge adults are usually tiny insects, the artificials we tie to suggest them are dressed on hook sizes ranging from 12 to 26, with 14s, 16s and 18s most predominant. Midge pupae, on the other hand, are usually somewhat larger than the adult insects they contain. For example, there's one relatively large midge that hatches in some regions during October and November, the adult form of which is best suggested on a size 14, 2XL hook. At hatching time the pupa of this midge compares in size to a size 10, 2XL hook.

When fish are feeding on midges at or slightly beneath the lake surface, they'll often "cruise" rapidly along, in an upwind direction if there's a riffle, quietly sucking the pupae from beneath the surface film and newly hatched adults from the surface. It isn't at all uncommon to find fish "head and tailing" when they're feeding on midge pupae beneath the surface of a lake. As the fish takes in the pupa from immediately beneath the surface film, the fish's nose will bulge or break the surface. Then, as the momentum of the movement carries the fish forward through the water and slightly downwards, the fish's tail disturbs the surface, all of which sometimes gives the impression of two rises. At other times the fish's nose will not break the surface leaving only a strange looking "shimmer" on the surface film sometimes accompanied by the tail breaking the surface. This type of rise is called "tailing" and varies in intensity from a silent slicing of the surface film by the tail to a relatively noisy splash. Generally, during periods when fish are feeding on hatching midge pupae they'll also be feeding on hatched adult midges, often with soft, though audible, "sucking" or "lip smacking" sounds.

Both casting and mooching methods can be employed effectively when fish are feeding on midges.

Leading the "Cruiser"

Although mooching nymphs near the surface on floating lines is highly productive during midge hatching periods, casting to cruising game fish is far more exciting and certainly a great deal more challenging. The angler first attempts to judge the direction, speed and frequency of the rises of the fish, then casts ahead of where the last rise occurred. He then imparts a slow retrieve, tensely waiting for that telltale twitch of the leader or swirl that denotes the fish has taken his artificial.

There are really no firm rules to follow when casting ahead of cruising fish, but most old hands at the game look for the fish's second or third rise to calculate both how fast the fish is swimming and the average distance between its rises (Fig. 53). The angler then makes a cast that will hopefully intersect the path of the feeding fish. If a strike is not forthcoming, the angler then looks for other rising fish on which to concentrate his efforts.

Although midging game fish frequently cruise upwind into a riffle or along the edge of a slick, the occasions are numerous when they feed in irregular or circular patterns in fairly restricted areas. On those occasions it's often necessary to cast your fly almost directly to each rise, allowing it to remain there until the fish finds it. Therefore, before you start casting to fish with midges on their minds, closely observe the pattern of the rises in order to determine whether or not to lead the fish.

Casting distances required for near-surface nymph fishing situations aren't usually as great as those necessary for achieving long, effective retrieves with deeply sunken artificials. With few exceptions, casts from 30 to 60 feet are adequate.

How game fish feed on hatching mayfly, dragonfly and damselfly nymphs is sometimes quite unlike the manner in which they seek out hatching midges. Where and how these nymphs crawl or swim to the surface to hatch pretty much determines the way game fish go after them. When the nymphs swim directly to the surface to hatch, you can expect to see the usual "bulging," "swirling" and "tailing" rises associated with nymphing fish. However, certain mayfly, dragonfly and damselfly nymphs crawl out of the water onto rocks, debris or aquatic plant stems *before* hatching. The depth at which the fish feed on *those* nymphs precludes much evidence of feeding activity. Of

 CAST HERE

 THIRD RISE

 SECOND RISE

 FIRST RISE

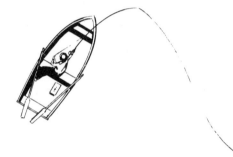

Fig. 53.   *How to "lead" cruising fish in a typical situation.*

course, experience will eventually sharpen one's intuitive powers to assess these occasions, but for starters, if you see insects hatching profusely, yet observe minimal surface activity on the part of the fish, it's a good idea to try fishing near the rocky shorelines or aquatic plants from which the insects are flying, using either floating or sink-tip fly lines.

By way of a review, mayfly nymphs are usually long-bodied creatures with two or three tails and external gills on their abdominal segments. Some mayfly nymphs burrow into and inhabit muddy lake bottom areas, like the midge larvae. Other more active "clambering" varieties of mayfly nymphs inhabit relatively hard lake bottoms. Normally, mayfly nymphs crawl out of the water onto rocks, reeds or aquatic plants before hatching into their adult forms. Then they shed their nymphal skins and enter the first of two distinctive adult developmental stages called the "dun." Depending on the species of the mayfly, this first stage lasts from a few minutes to several days, during which the insect's tails and legs grow longer and its reproductive system develops. Eventually, the mayfly dun sheds its entire skin and, following a mating flight (which usually occurs near or over the water), lays its eggs in the water, dying shortly thereafter.

Usually, the most productive times to seek out lake game fishes with mayfly nymph artificials are during brief periods immediately preceding hatches, when the nymphs are unusually active. These situations are not as difficult to predict as they are to observe, provided you know the approximate mayfly hatching "schedules" in a given lake. For example, March Brown mayflies almost invariably hatch out between May 8th and 20th at one of my favorite lakes. Several years of observing these March Brown hatches and recording their peculiarities in my log books have shown that most of the hatches occur between 11.00 A.M. and 1:00 P.M. Experience indicates that if I want to catch the fish from that lake on mayfly nymphs, I'm most likely to get results between 10.00 A.M. and noon, when the mayfly nymphs are actively crawling up the rocks to hatch on shore. After noon the fish almost invariably have begun to feed actively on adult duns, as they drift along in shimmering windrows next to the shoreline rocks. Once the hatch is well underway, it's usually necessary to switch to dry flies in order to continue catching trout.

Depending on the mayfly species hatching at a given moment, the most effective retrieve can vary from an absolutely "dead drift" to a very fast hand-twist. However, most lake mayfly species crawl and swim quite slowly. A relatively slow, methodical hand-twist retrieve, varied with occasional twitches imparted to the rod tip, will usually produce strikes. This slow retrieve is especially deadly on crappies.

Under this set of conditions, anchor very close to shore and cast the nymph on a floating line so it lands within inches of the rocks or reeds—places where the mayflies are likely to be crawling prior to the hatch. If you detect a telltale swirl, cast directly to the rings on the water or slightly beyond, allow the fly to sink for a moment, then start a slow, jerky retrieve. If you happen to be working an offshore reed or shoal area the same technique applies.

"Thinking like a fish" pays rich dividends in near-surface angling situations, as well as in all other forms of lake and stream fishing with flies. One of the most consistently successful nymph fishermen

I know, Joseph D. Miotke, proceeds on the theory that fish more readily accept nymphs retrieved in the same direction as the wind-drift on a lake than they do flies retrieved upwind. His method of anchoring downwind from the area he intends to fish, then casting directly up into or quartering across the wind invariably produces strikes when other methods fail, provided the fish are feeding, of course.

Naturally, there are times when fish can be coaxed into taking mayfly nymph fakes during periods not preceding hatches. Both deep-line and near-surface methods can be used successfully and sometimes entail literally crawling the fly along the lake bottom gravel, mud or debris.

Hosmer Lake in Oregon is an excellent place to observe how fish react to nymphs retrieved along the lake bottom. The 150-acre lake nestles at the foot of picturesque, snow-capped mountain peaks near the edge of the Three Sisters Wilderness area, some 32 miles from the community of Bend, Oregon. Hosmer Lake is a 4,950-foot high landlocked salmon paradise. Originally named "Mud Lake," Hosmer Lake was chemically treated in 1957 to eradicate populations of carp, roach and stunted brook trout. The salmon were introduced into the lake in 1958.

Hosmer Lake is actually two small lakes connected by a quarter-mile-long channel, both of which fall into the category of "shallow" bodies of water varying in depth from one to about 15 feet. White mud covers most of the lake bottom and rich, food-producing chara weeds promote the growth of myriads of aquatic insect nymphs and scuds.

Massive hatches of mayflies occur on Hosmer Lake sporadically from late spring throughout the summer, usually hitting their peak about the 4th of July. The landlocked salmon look with special favor on the nymphs and adults of the Black Drake mayfly which begins showing in June and continues to hatch in spurts practically throughout the summer according to local experts.

Neither the salmon nor the brook trout found in Hosmer Lake are so numerous one can make blind casts and expect frequent strikes. Each fish must be individually sought out in most instances.

Further complicating the fishing is the fact that virtually every salmon residing in Hosmer Lake has, at one time or another, felt the prick of a hook. The salmon fishing there is strictly for "fun." All salmon hooked must be released unharmed. And it's easy to see how, after a few unpleasant encounters with artificial flies, some of those lunker salmon become very wary of anglers' offerings.

You may spot a salmon, for example, and, noting no hatch is in progress, decide to try for him with a small dark nymph. The water in Hosmer Lake is extremely clear. A cast made directly to or over the fish, which may or may not be cruising in search of food, usually results in a response bordering on total indifference! However, cast your nymph from 10 to 20 feet ahead of the salmon, allow it to sink to the muddy lake bottom, twitch the fly through the mud, allowing it to kick up little white, underwater "clouds" and—watch out! Chances are you'll soon have a handful of bucking fly rod or a broken tippet! Close observation of the behavior of live nymphs in Hosmer Lake provides the answer to the salmons' behavior in this instance. The natural nymphs kick up little clouds of mud when they move rapidly, which in turn direct the attention of the fish to the nymphs.

A Special Opportunity

Most often lake fly fishermen tend to fish damselfly nymph imitations on sinking fly lines over weed beds in 10 to 20 feet of water, frequently ignoring occasions when similar artificials fished on floating or sink-tip lines would produce fantastic results.

Damselflies usually lay their eggs in the tissues of water plants. During the winter months the young, greenish or tan damselfly nymphs pass through as many as 15 developmental stages, during which time they increase in size and prey upon other insect larvae, most notably those of the mosquito. Hatching of the slender-bodied nymphs with the three paddlelike, tracheal gills tipping their abdomens usually begins in May in areas as northerly as Washington State, reaching a peak in June.

Because of the peculiar, wriggly manner in which damselflies wend their ways to the surface to hatch, it's usually necessary to impart some sort of jerky, rising motion to the artificial damselfly nymph during the retrieve. Weighted nymphs, fished on floating lines and long, fine leaders, are especially useful as the naturals approach the surface in shallow water. The nymph is cast out over the shallows, allowed to sink close to the bottom, then retrieved *upwards* by raising the rod tip with short, lifting jerks. At other times, an erratic, fast, hand-twist retrieve produces the fastest action.

Extremely large game fish often behave in ways that utterly confound fly fishermen. One of the most perplexing traits of large fish is their frequent unwillingness to move more than a few feet from their feeding stations. This frustrating habit is often compounded during periods when massive numbers of nymphs are on the move, as is the case during some damselfly hatches. Take the case of a favorite, rich 100-acre lake of mine over half of which consists of a shallow, weedy flat averaging three to six feet deep. The flat is an almost ideal place to fish nymphs on sink-tip or floating fly lines during insect hatches.

Managed on a "quality" fishing basis, with restricted catch limits, the lake consistently produces trout in the two- to six-pound class. However, this delightful body of water contains a superabundance of natural fish food organisms. The rainbows there can be very persnickety as a result. During damselfly hatches the lunker rainbows inhabiting the shallows very often refuse offerings that aren't behaving as do the natural nymphs, that is *rising* towards the surface.

I recall a day not long ago when some 50 fly fishermen, members of a large fly fishing club, were gathered for a social "fish out" at the lake. About midmorning the damselflies began to hatch. The tackle-busting 'bows went on the prod. Yet, out of that imposing number of anglers, many of whom were experienced lake fishing veterans, only two could plant barbs in fish flesh. Between them, they hooked and released so many large trout that some of the other fly fishermen made disparaging remarks!

The successful anglers drew upon their knowledge of the habits of large rainbow trout and their behavior during damselfly hatches to develop a killing method for the conditions of the moment. First, they cast only to the largest swirls they observed. They didn't waste time trying for small trout. Being well aware of the unwillingness of large trout to move far for food during massive insect hatches, they cast their nymph flies within a foot or two of each rise. Equally important, the successful fly fishermen retrieved only a few feet of line before making a new cast. Under those "lazy trout" conditions, they knew that the most effective retrieve was less than ten feet. The two anglers observed the damselfly nymphs wriggling their ways to the surface with vigorous lashing motions of their paddlelike gills. One of the chaps tried to simulate those motions of the naturals by jiggling the tip of his fly rod as he also lifted it to emulate the rising of the nymph through the water. Their relatively short retrieves, combined with jiggling lifts of their rod tips resulted in sensational success!

Consistent Killers

You may recall that the voracious, often fast-moving nymphs of the dragonfly undergo aquatic development similar to that of damselflies. The king-sized dragonflies commonly called "darning needles" (Family: *aeshnidae*) come from relatively large, elongate nymphs that propel themselves rapidly along through the water by ejecting water through their gill chambers. Other common dragonfly nymphs are more ovate in shape.

Most dragonfly nymph species are best suggested by large olive or brown colored fur or chenille bodied nymphs retrieved with fast strips on sinking fly lines. Although maximum dragonfly hatching activity occurs in the late spring, artificial dragonfly nymphs are highly effective throughout the calendar year.

When dragonfly hatching takes place in relatively shallow water, slow-sinking, sink-tip and floating lines can be effectively employed, the main difference in technique being the speed and type of retrieve. Certain species of game fish take such wicked cuts at properly retrieved dragonfly nymphs they hook themselves. Tippets testing four pounds or stronger are highly recommended when you're fishing dragonfly nymphs in waters containing large game fish.

Artificial caddis flies also require highly refined retrieves to be effective. You may recall from Chapter I that caddis flies (Order: *trichoptera*) are one of the most important foods of freshwater fishes. Lake-inhabiting species mate in flights over the water. Then the female caddis flies usually swim down to the lake bottom, attaching their eggs to submerged stones and vegetation. The young caddis spends the winter as a larval "worm," building a portable home around itself out of bits of sand, pieces of debris or vegetable matter pasted together in the form of a protective tube. Ultimately, the insect pupates within a cocoon inside the larval case. When development is complete, the pupa nips its way out of the cocoon, swims very slowly to the surface and hatches.

Four Very Distinct Techniques

Actually, when we speak of "fly fishing with caddis flies" we're talking about four distinct types of fishing: (1) slowly retrieving or trolling nymphs suggesting the caddis fly's encased larval worm along the lake bottom with a sinking line, (2) "dead-drifting" or mooching nymphs representing the caddis fly pupa as it rises towards the surface to hatch on either sinking, sink-tip or floating fly lines, (3) dry fly fishing with patterns that emulate the newly hatched caddis fly as it extends its wings high above its back, and (4) dry fly fishing with artificials shaped like adult caddis flies, with their wings folded "tent" style over their backs.

Near-surface nymph methods are most applicable to imitating the slow swimming of the caddis pupa to the surface, preparatory to hatching. Two methods have achieved degrees of popularity. Because of its ease, mooching with a floating, sink-tip or slow-sinking line is the most popular, though not necessarily the most effective of the two techniques. Under certain conditions, the most important of which is a light breeze, a more sophisticated angling method called "dead-drifting" can produce astonishing results.

Although simple to describe, the dead-drift requires *intense* concentration if results are to be expected. First, the boat is anchored over a shoal or shallow flat where caddis flies are known to hatch. Casts are made with a floating line and sometimes weighted nymph either up or quartering up and across the prevailing breeze. The nymph is then allowed to drift downwind without any further retrieve motions other than those supplied by wave action.

Close attention must be paid to the behavior of the line, rod tip and leader during the dead-drift. Often fish will take and eject the drifting nymph before the angler has time to set the hook. Polaroid sunglasses are also a substantial aid to dead-drift fishing when there is glare on the water. Polaroids sometimes assist you in actually seeing the flash from the side of a fish when it turns to take your nymph.

7

Dry
Fly Fishing

Dry fly fishing on lakes is basically much the same exercise it is on streams, with certain notable differences, some aspects being easier, others more difficult. Virtually every factor influencing one's "luck" in stream situations requiring the use of floating artificials ultimately has some bearing on similar lake fishing occasions. Manipulation of a floating artificial is probably the most important aspect affecting lake dry fly fishing.

Throughout this book you've studied the evolution of effective still-water angling techniques from first-hand observation and experimentation. And, as you develop killing retrieves of nymphs and streamer flies by emulating the movements of underwater creatures, you similarly evolve successful dry fly fishing methods by scrutinizing the movements of aquatic and terrestrial insects on the surface and attempting to impart similar movements to your floating fakes.

The relatively tiny midges have long tested the skills of professional and amateur fly dressers alike. It's no simple assignment to recreate a delicate, two-winged mosquitolike insect on a hook ranging down to as small as size 26, but it's often worth the effort! I recall

112

one evening when a friend and I hooked a half-dozen three- to five-pound landlocked salmon on size 22 midge imitations. And, my log books contain numerous references to occasions when a box of ultra-tiny dry flies saved the day!

Most of the midges large enough to represent on fly hooks rest motionless on the surface of the lake for several moments after hatching, waiting for their wings to dry before attempting flight. During that brief interval, a midge is a "sitting duck" for any hungry fish that happens along. Probably the most effective way to fish a midge dry fly is to cast it in front of a chain-feeding fish and allow it to remain motionless. It's a rare occasion when twitching or retrieving a dry midge adds substantially to its effectiveness. Actually, "working" a midge usually detracts from its inherent fish-appeal.

Mayflies, the most frequently represented artificials in many stream fishermen's boxes, can impact heavily on the lake angler's methods, especially during those spring and early summer periods of maximum hatching activity. Trout, bass and panfish all gobble mayflies from the surfaces of lakes with great gusto.

Certainly the most frustrating aspect of dry fly fishing lakes for the stream-oriented angling addict is learning whether or not to lead a rising fish, how far to lead the rise and whether or not to impart action to the fly. Hatches and mating flights of mayflies catalyze the problem into a nightmarish potion of variables, so much so that a man with military experience might be tempted to call it a "Chinese fire drill!"

There's little doubt lake fishermen would cuss less and catch more fish during times of mayfly activity if all mayflies behaved similarly after shucking off their nymphal cases. But, they don't. Mayfly species and subspecies are not only fairly numerous in certain lakes, but also highly variable in behavior after hatching. For example, some hatching duns, like those of the Yellow Drake, rest perfectly motionless, wings held erect over their backs until ready to fly away. Other mayflies hatch, then flex or flutter their wings within seconds of attaining adulthood. Egg-laying "spinners" can be a flurry of activity one moment and floating dead and spent the next. Even then efforts to suggest the movements of adult mayflies would be fairly simple if each mayfly species hatched at a time when no other insect types were active. But again, they don't—not always! I recall one day on a lake when two distinct species of mayfly were hatching, another species mating and dying, and thousands of blue damselflies hatching —simultaneously! Deciding how to fish a dry fly, what dry fly to use or whether it might be better to fish a near-surface nymph was, on that occasion (if you'll pardon the expression), a real bag of worms!

At other times, the fishing is much easier, such as one time when cutthroat and rainbow trout were feeding on hatching March Brown duns within inches of the rocky shoreline. A stiff breeze was blowing the hatching insects off bushes and rocks into the water, piling them in amber windrows into the slicks and pockets next to shore. The trout were having a field day!

One cast I made caused my dry fly to bounce off a rock and settle delicately into a bottle-shaped pool between the rocks. The artificial bobbed enticingly for a moment, then disappeared. I thought the wave action had drowned the fly and raised my rod tip.

There was a platter-sized swirl as a surprised rainbow reacted to the prick of the hook and pull of the line! My companion looked incredulously at me when I cautioned him to prepare to lift the anchor. Line was scorching off my reel.

"I've hooked a dandy, and I just remembered this reel hasn't any backing!" I exclaimed frantically.

"Ho! Come on! That's just a 'tiddler'," joked my friend, almost choking on his words when the obviously large trout soared out of the water at the end of a 20-yard long run.

"Another run like that, now, and I've had it," I moaned. "What's more, I'm using two-pound test tippet!"

He yanked up the anchor and quickly rowed towards the fish so I could gain back some much needed line. A little later we netted a gorgeous, deep-bodied rainbow that tipped the scales at four pounds, nine and a half ounces. It was a handsome fish, strongly spotted with black markings and with a deep crimson blush on its side.

About an hour later my friend cozied his dry fly into a similar niche between the rocks. The fly scarcely touched water before disappearing in a shower of spray! His big 'bow weighed four pounds, six ounces.

What About Selectivity?

It is usually during hatches or mating flights of several mayfly species that the trouts and sometimes bass most frequently exhibit that maddening aspect of their nature called "selectivity." Some of angling's most exacting researchers have failed to come up with completely demonstrable theories to explain the phenomenon. Therefore, I won't attempt to pool my ignorance with theirs and further confuse the issue. Certainly, only a fish itself could tell us the real reasons why he shows preference for one type of mayfly over another. But I've always suspected the answer is really far more simple than we fishermen would like to think. Perhaps it's nothing more than fish, like people, having developed "tastes" for certain species of insects over others. Perhaps some day a scientist will fully prove one of the present "theories," perhaps not. The fact remains that bass, rainbows, cutthroats, brookies, browns, arctic grayling and land-locked salmon do feed selectively at times. Once in a while we fishermen stumble on the fly that fools 'em.

For example, I know of a lake where the trout are so persnickety during hatches of Black Drakes they'll virtually ignore artificials tied with *dyed* black hackle, yet go "ape" over those dressed with *natural* black hackles. And, who would think that so seemingly an insignificant factor as the difference in color between a yellow or tan rib on a March Brown dry fly would make a difference? It has, and does— in a significant manner recorded over several seasons of fishing! Then of course there are those utterly inexplicable moments when the fish willingly take in *any* artificial fly from a size 18 Black Midge to a size 6 White Miller—right smack in the middle of a heavy hatch of Green Drakes.

If you think fish behavior as influenced by adult mayflies is confusing—give airborne damselflies a try! Probably the ultimate frustration in a fly fisherman's life is a futile attempt to attract fish whose eyes are focused *above* the water on hovering damselflies. How does one copy the actions of a flying insect? Short of constructing a two-inch long helicopter and dressing it in feathers, he doesn't! No known manipulation has been demonstrated 100 percent effective when game fish are zeroing in on hovering damselflies. Certainly, an occasional fish will rise to a reasonable imitation of a damselfly twitched erratically on the surface. But, the times are few when this method produces consistent results when the fish—especially rainbow trout —are picking the insects out of the air. Bass, on the other hand, are less prone to feed on hovering damselflies to the exclusion of all other aquatic creatures. The bass seldom care whether or not an insect is hovering or struggling on the surface.

Artificials suggesting fast-flying adult dragonflies are usually so bulky and wind-resistant as to discourage their use on light trout tackle. However, artificial dragonflies can be extremely deadly when fished for bass and pike in a struggling manner on the surface with rods powerful enough to handle the heavy lines necessary to cast them effectively.

The creations we whip together to suggest adult caddis flies are fairly easy to manipulate. Adults of some caddis fly species, like the famed "Traveling Sedge" of interior British Columbia, pop out of their pupae at the surface and momentarily extend their wings vertically over their backs, rather like Yellow Drake duns. Sometimes an adult caddis will flap its wings immediately after hatching, before the membranes have dried, become airborne for a moment, then fall heavily back onto the surface where it will then scurry around, wings folded in the customary "tent" fashion over its back. The frantic surface wanderings of newly hatched caddis flies resulted in their being nicknamed "Traveling Sedges."

Fly fishermen have thus far developed two extremely effective techniques to represent newly hatched caddis flies on lakes. The first method incorporates an all-deer hair "bug" called the "Tom Thumb" which suggests the caddis with its wings raised into a vertical position. Usually, the Tom Thumb dry fly is fished dead in the water, with only an occasional twitch of the rod tip to suggest life.

The second method employs a large dry fly dressed in the tent-wing style. One of the most effective flies of this type is the "Salmon Candy" (page 158). Tent-winged caddis artificials are usually best fished by allowing them to rest motionless for a moment on the surface, then skittering them erratically along with movements of the rod tip, pausing periodically to let them remain still.

My dad and I recently used both methods with rare success at an outstanding mountain lake. The caddis flies were unseasonally late in hatching. We fished for ten days without observing a significant sedge hatch. To compound the matter, the moon was coming into its "full" phase. When that happens in connection with nocturnal sedge hatches the fish sometimes feed all night long.

We decided to fish until we became too sleepy to continue casting, on the chance the sedges were hatching at later than normal hours. Usually the hatch begins anywhere between sundown and 9:00 P.M. Occasionally, the sedges hatch during the daytime hours.

On the evening in question, not a single sedge "popped," as our

Canadian friends say, until about 9:30 P.M. Then a heavy fish swirled off the point of an island, at the edge of a slick and a wind riffle. Soon other fish boiled to the surface. In the clear moonlight we could see the silhouettes of newly hatched sedges, wings raised vertically, and the V-shaped trails of others of their kind traveling along the surface. During the first few minutes of the hatch we hooked and released several hefty battlers on Tom Thumb dry flies, fished dead in the water. But, as more and more of the hairy-winged insects came forth from the silvery blackness, the fish zeroed in on the "travelers," and we were forced to switch to down-wing dry flies. All the fish that didn't break our tippets on the strike, or cast free our hooks during jumps, were released unharmed. It was an incredible evening I shall never forget!

Game fish take into their gullets an amazing variety of aquatic and terrestrial life. I've actually observed largemouth bass and northern pike waylay creatures as large as ducklings! But by and large, most of the terrestrials taken in as fish foods are somewhat smaller than ducklings, usually insects like bees, ants and grasshoppers, or frogs, snakes and rodents that have been blown into the water by the wind, or otherwise hop, fall or slither into the water.

Ants and grasshoppers rank high on the list or common terrestrial insects eaten by game fishes. Massive mating flights of flying ants are fairly common during late May and early June where I do a great deal of lake fishing in the spring. You can imagine how the trout and bass respond when all of a sudden thousands of ants fall into the water en masse! At times it seems as though every fish in the lake goes on the prod. When these exciting, though infrequent angling windfalls occur, the need for finesse of presentation and retrieve usually goes out the window. I recall one occasion when I hooked and released a fish on virtually every cast during a two-hour period when an ant mating flight descended on a favorite lake in June. About all a fellow needed to catch fish that day was a black fly that vaguely resembled an ant.

Glowing late summer and early fall days occasionally provide similar fly fishing delights when a gusty breeze blows enough grasshoppers into the lake to excite the fish to a frenzy. Under these conditions the bass, trout and panfish often seem to lose most of their instinctive caution, feeding eagerly on virtually anything the appropriate size, shape and color of a hopper.

Nature sometimes provides an additional exciting bonus to lake fly fishermen when large numbers of bees and wasps occasionally swarm out over the lake on a frosty fall day, run out of "gas," and "ditch" in the "drink." Virtually any insectivorous game fish will eat a fallen bee on occasion, but the strain of cutthroat trout found between the eastern slopes of the Cascade range and the western slopes of the Rocky Mountains literally go wild over them!

One chill, bright September 25th on Priest Lake, Idaho, when bees by the hundreds flew to their aquatic Waterloo in the bay where I was fishing, dozens of cutthroat trout zeroed in on the struggling hymenopterae. All you had to do to get strikes was cast out a size 10 Western Bee bucktail floater, let it rest motionless on the water and wait until one of the hungry trout found it. A dozen cutthroats from ten inches to three and a half pounds spotted my fly that morning. I released all but three; one fish weighing nearly four pounds.

Big Flies for Big Fish

Of all the outlandish variety of creatures gobbled up by muskies, bass and pike from the surfaces of lakes, three are especially well suited to representation by artificial flies and fly fishing methods: mice, frogs and moths. There's scarcely a self-respecting bass or pike that can't be suckered into pouncing on a deer hair "bug" resembling a moth, mouse or frog. This isn't pushover fishing like one can experience on a cutthroat lake during an ant flight. Bass, especially, are wary—altogether as keen-eyed and cautious as brown trout, if not more so! And if you've never been exposed to bass fishing, there are some insights into bass "psychology" you should be aware of.

Being a predacious, omnivorous "critter" that will stuff almost any creature up to the size of a baseball into his maw, one might conclude catching bass on surface bugs would be a snap. But, bass are suspicious by nature, and their eyesight is so keen as to catalyze that suspicion into out and out fear at times. When a small land animal, snake or large insect falls noisily into the water near a bass, the bass becomes frightened momentarily and darts away. If the fish hasn't been too badly frightened by the initial splash he'll sometimes stop a few yards away and look back at where the commotion took place. After a while, sometimes as long as five or ten minutes, the bass will forget his fright and become curious, for he is a predator and anything falling into the water to him could mean "food." The bass will sometimes swim back to where the ruckus took place. If the bass then observes some filling morsel like a mouse struggling helplessly on the surface—pity the mouse! But if that object happens to be a well-designed deer hair mouse—pity the bass!

Northern pike and muskies, although often moody creatures, have little to fear from anything entering the water near them. When a deer-hair bug is cast anywhere within a few yards of a pike, allowed to remain motionless until the ripples subside, then twitched slowly, chances are a pike'll nail it with a rush, provided he's in the mood to feed.

Muskies, on the other hand, are less predictable. Those who fish for them a great deal sometimes refer to them as totally unpredictable. But, when the mood to feed near the surface strikes him, this spectacular giant can provide you with some heart-pounding thrills on surface flies.

Two of us once hooked pike from six to 15 pounds on almost every cast during three hours of fly fishing. Once we located a bay teeming with pike we cast out deer-hair moths, allowing them to rest motionless on the water, which ran from three to 20 feet deep. About half the time the pike would attack our bugs before we could start retrieves.

Before we leave the subject of floating artificials, there are certain lake areas where you can most effectively score with what could be considered stream fishing techniques. For example, take the case of a large lake outlet where fish food organisms are washed from the lake into the river or stream, sometimes concentrating game fish in that portion of the river immediately downstream from where it exits the lake.

At first glance one might be tempted to fly fish such an area by dropping anchor and casting, allowing a dry or wet fly to drift downstream cross current. Provided the area is navigable, another approach is suggested. Wouldn't it be possible to eliminate virtually all "drag" from the dry fly by casting directly downstream from the boat and floating over the prospective hot spots? From the standpoint of the game fish such a drag-free presentation would bring the artificial to them in virtually the same way the current carries along natural insects. Both methods in practice have merit. Which one you select will ultimately be determined by the species of game fish inhabiting the outlet and types of natural foods available to them.

At one of my favorite lakes a very large river exits the main lake at a spot several hundred yards wide at a speed varying between two and eight knots. The water is deep enough to accommodate motor-powered boats. Hybrid rainbow-cutthroat trout, rainbow trout, white-fish and salmon all are attracted to the two-mile long run imme-diately downstream from the outlet proper. The fish inhabiting this aquatic "bottleneck" feed actively on hordes of shrimps, mayflies, caddis flies and an abundance of terrestrial insects.

When the fish are feeding primarily on the light-sensitive shrimps, near the surface at dusk and later, the most effective way to work the area is from a drifting boat with a wet fly fished on a short line directly downstream. However, once the fish home in on float-ing mayflies and caddis it's usually as productive to anchor and cast near known feeding stations as it is to float.

The subject of dry fly fishing in the environment of the stream has been so thoroughly examined in multitudes of fine books it is unnec-essary to dwell at great length here on the subject of delicacy of delivery and the cautious, quiet approach to feeding game fish. Those are fundamental to virtually all conditions requiring the use of float-ing flies. It would be equally wasteful of your time and mine to dwell on the importance of sinking the dry fly tippet below the surface film of the water. Floating tippets on unruffled lake and stream waters produce adverse reactions to our floating artificials in wary species of game fish. I mention them here only to refresh your memory of these basics of fly fishing.

A delicate delivery of the fly is the product of one's casting exper-tise and well balanced terminal tackle. Cautious approach is achieved by either drifting, wading or rowing quietly to within casting distance. And, as for a sinking leader, few of the commercial preparations pres-ently available to promote sinking are 100 percent effective. The best ones are usually "goos" dinged-up out of a plumbing compound called "Bentonite" and some sort of binding agent. I've had good results by adding Bentonite to some of the commercial, paste-type leader sinking preparations. Fly leaders specially treated to sink were re-cently introduced commercially.

8

Fly

Casting

Basic fly casting is neither hard to understand nor exceptionally difficult to learn. In reality, we do not cast "flies," but fly lines, which in effect act as weights. The weight of the fly line affects the action of a fly rod in much the same way as the weight of a lure influences a spinning rod or casting rod.

To begin with, take your fly rod and attach a one-quarter-ounce weight (a sinker will do) to the tip guide with a string or piece of monofilament leader material. Hold the rod in a horizontal plane. Notice the amount of bend the sinker puts into the rod. Now, take a five-eighths-ounce sinker and attach it to the rod tip. Observe how much more additional bend the heavier weight puts into the rod. The weights of various fly lines similarly affect fly rods. Each fly rod is designed to deliver its maximum amount of thrust, or "power," under the influence of a specific amount of weight. Precisely how much weight brings out the optimum performance of rods designed for fly casting varies from fly rod to fly rod just as it does with various models of spinning and bait casting rods. If a certain fly line is too light for a specific rod it will not cause the rod to flex enough to deliver its maximum thrust. On the other hand, if the line is too heavy for the rod, it will overload the rod, causing it to lose some of its power delivering capabilities. But, if the weight of a line fully brings out the maximum casting power inherent in a given rod, that rod and that line are said to be "balanced."

An experienced fly caster can usually tell if a line and rod are in balance simply by casting with them for several minutes. Novice casters are advised to take careful note of the rod manufacturer's recommendations for line weight. Suggested line weights are usually marked on fly rod butt sections slightly forward of the cork grip. A beginning caster will be unable to learn to cast properly with a rod and line in severe imbalance. The really skilled caster can probably cast 30 to 50 feet of forward taper line without using a rod at all!

The secret to effective fly casting is to keep the rod "loaded" with the weight of the fly line throughout both the backward and forward casting motions. By keeping the weight of the line in constant inter-action with the flexing and unflexing of the rod you are not only capable of controlling the direction of the cast, but also in a position to impart sufficient speed to the line to thrust it backwards and forwards.

Casting's Basic Principle

Visualize the fly line and its weight as an integral part of your fly rod. By forming a mental picture of rod and line as a single unit it's easier to understand one of the fundamental principles of fly casting: the line goes where the rod tip goes. If you lift the rod tip briskly upwards, the line *must* travel in an upward direction. Jerk the rod tip sharply to your rear and the line *must* travel rapidly in that direc-tion. Drive the rod tip forward and you'll invariably propel the line forward. Why, even if you jiggle the rod tip back and forth as you drive line forward, the line *must* travel along a similar, wavy tra-jectory.

Now, let's put together a basic cast. The first part of the fly cast consists of making the line airborne. Strip out approximately 20 feet of your weight-forward, tapered fly line. Extend the line straight ahead of you on the grass. With the rod tip held at slightly below the ten o'clock position in front of you, very rapidly, smoothly and

Fig. 54. *Backcast and forward cast in three steps: (1) Lift rod tip sharply to 2 o'clock; (2) start forward thrust of rod when line straightens; (3) stop rod tip at 10 o'clock, then follow through toward target.*

firmly lift and accelerate the rod tip, stopping it abruptly at the one o'clock position over your shoulder (Fig. 54). This is the basic movement of the back-cast. It is accomplished with a short, firm, rapidly accelerating lift of hand, arm and shoulder until the casting hand reaches a point approximately opposite your ear. At this point, forearm, wrist and rod should be in an almost straight line with one another. The wrist should not be bent towards the rear or canted either to the left or the right. If you bend your wrist you will cause the rod tip to subscribe a path backwards and downwards, carrying the line along with it. You want the line to travel *up* and back from the rod tip. The wrist must be kept very firm during the back-cast in order to maintain absolute control over the arc subscribed by the rod tip. If you happen to be a golfer you will instantly recognize the similarity of principle between the back swing of golf and back-cast of fly fishing. The mechanics are quite different, but the principal objective, controlling the path subscribed by club or rod tip, is the same.

If you happen to be a veteran angler who learned his casting technique in the school advocating holding a handkerchief next to your side under your casting arm during practice sessions, forget about it! That style of casting may perform beautifully on small streams. But for the really long casts you'll sometimes need to make on lakes you'll have to retrain your entire casting hand, arm and shoulder. To make the power casts arm and elbow must be held away from the body as they are in pounding with a hammer. The elbow and upper arm are held almost 90 degrees horizontally from the torso.

Make some more back-casts. Practice nothing else until each back-cast you make soars *upwards* and backwards.

Now, let's go on to the next step. As the fly line unfurls up and back, then drops through an arc of about 45 degrees, you'll feel it pulling on your rod tip, loading the rod with weight. When you see the line begin to straighten out behind you, the loading of the rod during the back-cast will be at its maximum. Therefore, slightly *before* the line is fully extended, rapidly thrust the rod tip forward to a point slightly above ten o'clock (Fig. 54). The forward casting motion of hand, arm and shoulder should resemble the physical movements used to drive a nail with a hammer. If you have performed both the back-cast and forward cast properly, the rod will drive the line straight out to a point in the air that is just about 20 feet ahead of you.

Grip and Squeeze

I've delayed discussing the proper "grip" you take on your fly rod until now, because grip articulates intimately with the first refinement of casting we'll discuss—"squeeze." First, let me point out that although there are several effective ways to grip a fly rod the one described here will allow you to impart with relative ease the tremendous speed to the line necessary for making long casts. Other grips will accomplish the same end, but usually with far more strain and fatigue to the casting hand. Now grasp the cork grip with your casting hand like you would when shaking hands with someone. Notice that your thumb is probably resting along the upper, inner side of the cork grip. Next, shift the position of the thumb so that it rests comfortably on top of the cork rings (Fig. 55). Your hand is now in the most effective position to squeeze the grip. It is by *squeezing* the rod grip that we attain firmness of hand, wrist and forearm and ultimately transmit power to the rod and speed to the line. Let's apply the squeeze to some casts.

As you accelerate the rod tip upwards into a back-cast, squeeze the rod grip. Notice how much more additional force is applied to the rod and transmitted to the line! As the line starts to straighten out behind you, start the forward cast with a second, very firm

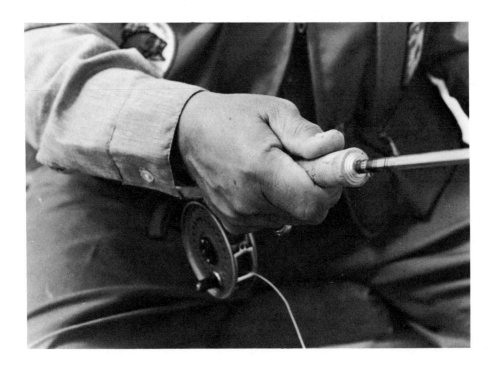

Fig. 55. *This is the correct grip.*

squeeze. The rod seems to spring alive in your hand, imparting almost unbelievable speed to the line with a minimum of effort on your part.

Try another cast. This time keep the line in the air through several consecutive back-casts and forward casts. Each time you lift the rod tip for a back-cast, squeeze the cork rings then *relax* your grip slightly as the line flows out behind you. Each time you drive the rod tip forward, squeeze the grip and follow through with a little push, like you were pushing open a door with your closed fist.

The "Bow"

As you continue casting backwards and forwards you may notice that the loop-shaped path described by the line is relatively narrow or tight. This loop in the line is called the "bow." When the bow is cast to describe the narrow oval pattern you are now hopefully casting, it is called a "tight bow" (Fig. 56). The tight bow is useful to make long distance casts and to drive a line into the teeth of a wind or stiff breeze. However, the tight bow does not promote especially delicate delivery of a fly.

In order to present a dry fly or small nymph with great finesse in relatively calm air you'll need to learn how to widen the bow in the

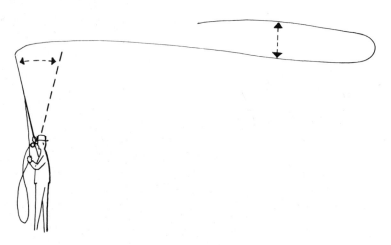

Fig. 56. *Tight bow. Note the narrow arc in which the rod is swung, and the narrow loop.*

line (Fig. 57). Let's go back to that basic principle: the line goes where the rod tip goes. To widen the bow in the line you simply need to widen the arc through which the rod tip passes. On this next series of practice casts start with the rod tip slightly below the 9:30 position. During the back-cast carry the thrust of the rod tip back slightly lower to approximately two o'clock. As you drive forward into the forward cast make a concerted effort to apply the power with the middle or butt section of the rod, instead of the tip.

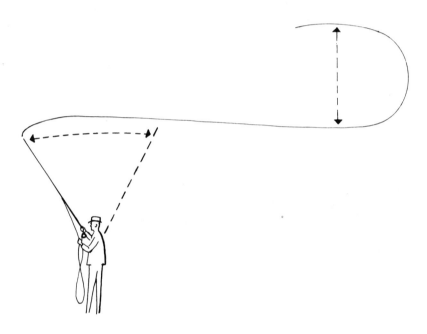

Fig. 57. *Wide bow, with wide arc of rod and wide loop of line.*

"Shooting" Line

Let's now take a long stride toward becoming an effective caster. Using the basic fly cast with the tight bow, cast to a spot some 30 feet distant. Strip an additional ten feet of line from your reel. Holding firmly to the line with the fingers of your retrieve hand, make another cast. When the line straightens out in front of you, release your grip on the remaining line. Watch that additional line "shoot" out through the guides and lengthen your cast. Make another cast. With 30 to 35 feet of line beyond the rod tip, uncoil 20 additional feet of line from the reel. Take care to make your back-cast quite high and to squeeze firmly during both back and forward casts. All 20 feet of additional line should shoot out smoothly through the guides. Try it again, this time using 35 feet of line to make the basic cast while attempting to shoot an additional 35 to 40 feet of line. Chances are this cast will fall somewhat short of your expectations. Insufficient line speed is the probable reason you failed to cast 70 to 75 feet.

Turning on the Power

Here's where you learn to turn on the power! The line speed required to propel a line in excess of 75 feet is imparted with your *retrieve* hand, not your casting hand. You now have 70 to 75 feet of line off the reel, part of it beyond the rod tip, some of it coiled loosely at your feet. Coil all but 30 to 35 feet of the line at your feet. Now, grasp the line near the butt guide with the fingers of your retrieve hand. As you begin your back-cast with a squeeze and a lift, *pull down sharply* on the line held in your retrieve hand (Fig. 58). Notice how this downward hauling on the line imparts tremendous additional speed to the back-cast.

As the line zips back into the air and loads the rod tip with weight,

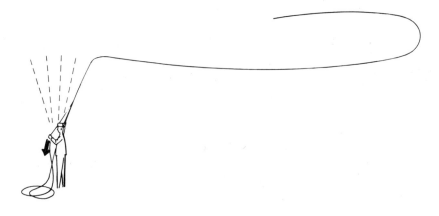

Fig. 58. *Diagram of a double-haul, lift. Pull down sharply as you make the back-cast lift.*

let the hand holding the line drift up towards the butt guide once again (Fig. 59). Now, start the forward cast by simultaneously squeezing and driving forward with your casting hand and making a second,

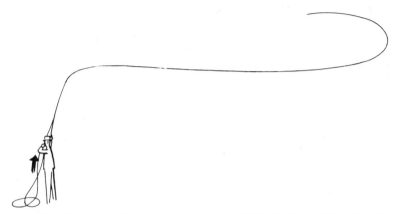

Fig. 59. *Diagram of a double-haul hand drift. Left hand holding line drift up as line travels up and back.*

sharp downward haul of the line held in your retrieve hand (Fig. 60). This second haul on the line loads the rod (bends it) to the point where it can unleash its maximum thrust, causing the line to flow forward at tremendous speed.

Finally, just before the bow in the line straightens out in front of

Fig. 60. *Applying the power in a double haul. Pull down sharply on line as you drive rod tip forward.*

you, release your grip on the line in the retrieve hand. The entire 70 to 75 feet of line should shoot out over the water and "hit" or come taut on the reel drum before settling to the water.

Eventually, by learning to keep your rod loaded with line weight during two or three false casts, slightly lengthening the line during those false casts, you should be able to train yourself to shoot an entire 90-foot fly line, with little real physical effort.

Refinement Takes Practice

Naturally, the basic techniques of casting you learn here will require considerable refinement in order to put them to the most effective use in actual fishing situations. Casting finesse is acquired during long hours of practice during which your casting hand and timing become finely tuned to perform the delicate variations in controlling a fly line that distinguish the polished caster from the neophyte. The same holds true for other sports requiring physical coordination. There simply is no short cut method by which you can become an "instant expert." The degree of casting proficiency you attain will depend on your ability to coordinate body movements and your willingness to refine them.

Two additional casting techniques come to mind that will assist you in becoming a proficient lake fly fisherman. Even nonfishermen have been acquainted with those valiant though noisily futile efforts of fly fishermen who slap the water with the line on the back-cast and "rip" the water to a froth when lifting the line from the water to begin casts. The cartoonists and jokesters have worked that subject into the ground. I can't honestly agree it's a mortal sin to occasionally tick the water behind you on a back-cast. After all, who fishes behind himself? What difference does it make if the line or fly does hit the water once in a while? Excessively disturbing the water over feeding fish in the direction in which we cast is an entirely different matter.

For that reason, let me suggest you learn how to make a "roll-cast pickup" of line, leader and fly from the water. First, raise your rod tip to the 12 o'clock position, so there is a large "belly" of line hanging from rod tip to the lake's surface in front of you (Fig. 61). Then, sharply drive your rod tip down and forward to about the nine o'clock position. The line will roll forward, break the surface tension

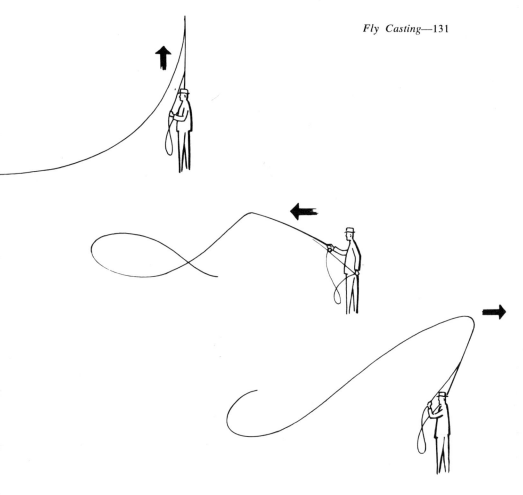

Fig. 61. *Roll-cast lift. First, raise rod tip to 12 o'clock position; second, drive rod tip smartly forward to a spot well over target; third, as line straightens out over water, snatch line up into normal backcast.*

holding it to the water and you can snatch it smartly into a normal back-cast with a minimum of disturbance to the surface.

Some lake fishing situations are most easily handled by casting with the other hand or making a "backhand" cast with your regular casting hand. An ability to cast effectively with either hand is espec- ially useful if you fish with a companion in a small boat. Some of us are so hopelessly committed to performing most of life's vital functions with one hand it isn't worth the effort to train that incredibly useless "other hand." Others take to ambidextrous casting with little effort.

For those afflicted with singular sinistrality here is how to accomplish the backhand cast (Fig. 62). Raise your casting arm and rod to a position parallel to the water, even with your chest.

Fig. 62. *Back-hand cast is approximately at 45-degree angle over opposite shoulder.*

The backhand cast employs essentially the same movements as a normal cast, except that the rod travels in a plane angled over your off-hand shoulder. Special care should be taken to hold the backcast quite high during a backhand cast. Some casters tend to drop their back casts excessively when attempting this off-hand form of delivery; resulting in unduly sloppy forward casts.

Casting a "Straight" Line

Casting a straight line is another problem that sometimes plagues the inexperienced caster. Fortunately, this casting fault is quite easy to correct. A line that lands crookedly on the water is usually the result of the angler "overshocking" his rod tip sometime during the forward cast. Recall that basic casting rule about "where the line goes?" If the final application of power to the rod tip is made in a jerky or overly forceful manner, resulting in the rod tip vibrating up and down at the completion of the casting motion the line will follow suit. Only trial and error practice will show you exactly when to deliver the maximum power thrust and how much zip to put into it. However, if you'll remember effective casting hinges more on *smoothness* and timing than on raw application of power, chances are you'll have little difficulty in piecing together an integrated, well-coordinated cast.

Coping with the Wind

A third and final factor will influence your casting on lakes: wind. You'll encounter wind coming from any one of four main directions, and sometimes, even from more than one direction at a time.

Wind from behind is probably the easiest to cope with. Just remember to throw your back-cast with sufficient extra force to drive out and straighten the line behind you. Otherwise, you'll probably experience the painful stab of a hook penetrating your ear, scalp, neck or eyebrow. When I was learning to fly cast as a lad I can recall one occasion when a hook was surgically removed from my fanny!

A direct head wind is also fairly easy to handle. Start out by making a relatively high back-cast with a tight bow. On the forward cast, however, instead of driving your rod tip forward to the ten o'clock position above the water, use a double-haul and aim the cast at a point a few feet short of your actual target, delivering the forward cast with very sharp thrust and follow through of the rod tip. The line should knife through the wind in a very tight bow that races forward barely above the surface of the lake, depositing the fly somewhere near the target. The wind tends to lift the line as the bow unfurls into its force, thus the reason for aiming short of the intended point of delivery (Fig. 63).

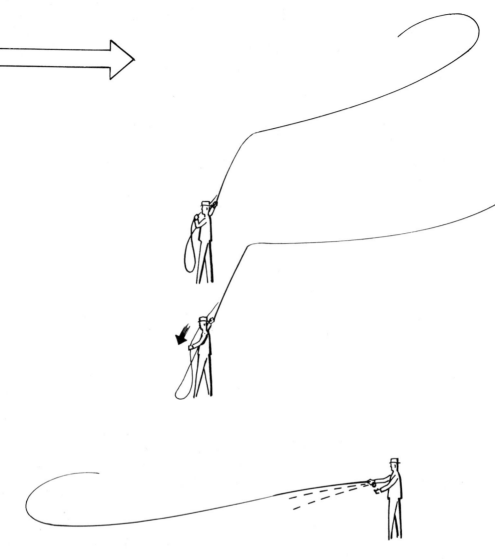

Fig. 63. *Headwind cast. First, make normal high back-cast, using a double-haul; second, start forward cast with very firm haul; third, drop rod tip to 9 o'clock position and follow through to a point short of target. Complete down-haul and shoot line as loop straightens out over water.*

Crosswind quartering or driving straight down on your casting arm can be both hazardous and difficult to cope with. I can't honestly recommend the following method of handling crosswind unless you are a skilled and readily adaptable caster to begin with. The technique requires sharp timing, a deft "touch" and an extremely watch-ful eye.

In this cast, first deliver the back-cast with a wide bow and much speed and firmness, momentarily stopping the rod tip at the one o'clock position. Then, in an almost continuous motion, allow the rod tip to "drift" back until the rod is extended behind you almost parallel to the water (Fig. 64).

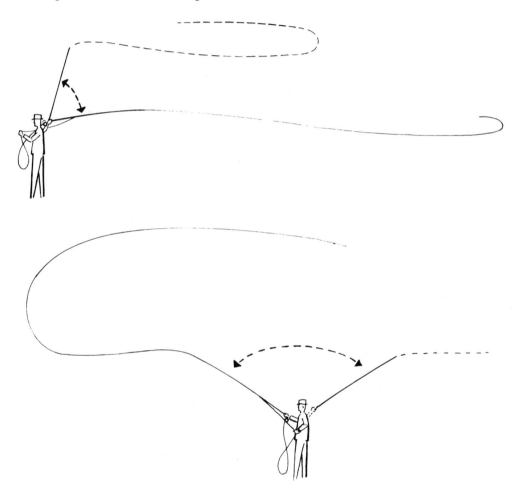

Fig. 64. *Cross-wind cast. At top, note wide arc. Allow rod tip to drift back almost parallel to water. Below, apply power with middle and butt of rod only, to "roll" line forward in very wide bow. Fly should remain above head level throughout cast.*

Deliver the forward cast to a point somewhat above the usual ten o'clock position, applying most of the power to the cast with the middle and butt sections of your rod. The extremely wide, rather sloppy looking bow thus created will roll the line forward over the top of your head or downwind shoulder. You'll be amazed not only by the considerable distances you can cast this way, but also by the beautiful manner in which line, leader and fly turn over at the completion of the cast.

9

Hooking and Landing Fish

Detecting the takes of game fish and hooking them in lakes can be extremely tricky, in some cases far more difficult than in streams. Many of the problems we encounter while attempting to plant our barbs firmly in the mouths of lake fishes emanate from the parabola-shaped "belly" formed in a sinking fly line as it descends deeper and deeper into the water (Fig. 65). In essence, the deeper the line sinks the less direct our connection to the fly becomes, reducing our ability not only to "feel" light strikes, but also to set the hook quickly.

Setting the hook in the mouth of a fish in water from 10 to 30 feet deep often requires intense concentration, sensitive "touch" and sharply honed reflexes. This is especially true when you're fishing deeply sunken nymphs for game fish that often merely "bump," "nudge," "tick" or "suck" at an artificial. Rainbow and cutthroat trout, crappies, bluegills and walleyes are the most common offenders.

There are several techniques we can use to aid us in detecting and capitalizing on the delicate feeding habits of game fishes. Positioning the rod tip within a few inches of the water's surface is a great way

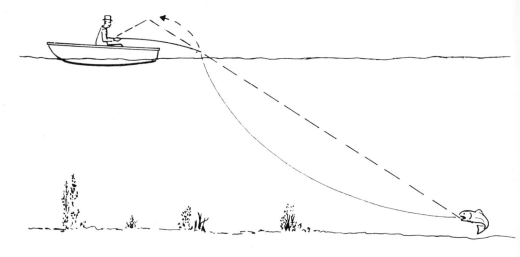

Fig. 65. *It is fairly easy to set hook with sinking line. Do it firmly, and keep rod tip close to water during retrieve. Note "belly" in line.*

to improve one's ability to "feel" light takes by fish. It also puts the rod tip in excellent position to set the hook with a rapidly accelerating, sideways movement similar in force and speed to the beginnings of a back-cast. The rod tip *must* travel far enough and fast enough to take up the belly of the sunken line before the fish has time to eject the fly. It takes a little experimentation to learn how to set the hook with a sinking line. If you apply excessive force to the strike you'll probably break your tippet. Set the hook too lightly and you'll no doubt miss the fish. The best advice I can give you is to make a habit of setting the hook *firmly* and *quickly* at the slightest hint of resistence to your fly.

Both problems are simplified as we fish our flies nearer to the surface. A sudden twitch or tightening of line or leader, a visible "flash" beneath the surface, a "bulge" or swirl in the water in the vicinity of the fly, or a well-defined tug are the most common signals that game fish have succumbed to the enticements of our nymph flies fished near the surface. Provided your hooks are sharp, setting the hook in any of these situations, as well as when a fish clobbers a dry fly, rarely requires more than a quick, firm tightening of the line. Unless you're fishing for hard-mouthed species like pike or bass, there's no need to sock home the hook with the degree of authority used to straighten the belly in a sinking line. A quick tightening up is usually more than adequate. But, when you're after muskies, pike or bass, use heavy tippets—eight- to 20-pound test—depending on the amount of "horsing" you may have to do. For pike and muskies add an additional three feet of 40- to 60-pound test "shock tippet" to accommodate for the sharp teeth. And, when you set the hook, really "whang" it home. In the case of a really large pike or musky I'll set the hook two or three times! I want to be absolutely certain that if my hook encounters bone, I set hard enough to penetrate it. I've even switched to the ultrahard, stainless steel saltwater hooks for my pike fishing. File the hook points to triangular shape to give three "cutting edges" to penetrate hard mouth parts.

A lot of beautiful trophy-sized game fish are lost because the angler panicked and tried to "horse" in the fish. Horsing is an essential technique in the landing of heavy pike and bass hooked in stump, brush and lily pad choked areas. But if you're going to pour the coal to a fish, be prepared for it with adequately strong leaders and large, heavy wire hooks that will bite deeply and bear the strain.

In the case of the stronger, fast-moving trouts and landlocked salmon, horsing is simply out of the question except in obstruction filled waters. The relatively fine tippets and light hooks sometimes necessary to coaxing these fish into strikes simply won't allow for mistakes in fish-handling!

Actually, common sense dictates the correct way to play a fish. Here's the formula: (1) Know your tackle. Be certain of the strength of your leader tippet before making that first cast. (2) Once you've hooked the fish feel free to apply all the pressure your tackle will bear, provided the fish is not in the process of jumping or moving rapidly in the opposite direction. (3) If a fish jumps, immediately drop your rod tip toward the surface of the water. Otherwise, if the fish falls back on your tippet the sudden stress may either tear the hook out of the fish's mouth or break the tippet. (4) If a fast-moving fish like a rainbow trout suddenly takes off on a fast run, let him run! You can't stop him! When the fish stops, immediately resume putting on the pressure with the rod. During an extremely long, fast run, point the rod tip directly at the fish. Your reel should be set just tight enough to keep it from "overrunning." A rod raised at a high angle during a run has the same effect as tightening the drag on your reel.

Now and then a trout or salmon will race directly towards your boat after being hooked. This is the one time you should *not* play the fish directly off the reel. Strip in line as fast as you can. Allow the line to fall in loose coils at your feet or into your stripping basket. When the fish has passed and is once again heading away from you, resume playing him off the reel.

Correct Netting Technique

At the risk of being called opinionated, I'm going to state flatly there are only two ways to net fish—the right way, which is head first into the net, and the wrong way, which may be any other technique one might conceivably contrive to reduce his trophy to possession, with the obvious exceptions of "tailing" salmon and the sporty "hand landing" method. Netting fish of any species is ridiculously easy provided you first play the creature down to where you can control it. When the fish is ready for landing, simply submerge the net bag and lead the fish into it head first. Then lift the net smoothly and quickly out of the water and into the boat. That's all there is to it!

If you intend to release the fish you catch, then pinch down or file off the barbs on your hooks. Barbless hooks are available in some tackle shops and through certain mail-order firms. Barbless hooks eliminate the necessity of bringing the fish aboard your boat and reduce the chances of fatally injuring your sporting prize. If the fish you intend to release appears to be distressed and unable to swim away under its own power, cradle it gently in your hands in the water until it regains its equilibrium and some strength. That carefully released battler might give you pleasure another day.

10

Boating
Safety
And Guides

Although this book is primarily concerned with fishing techniques it would be remiss on my part to neglect making a few comments about safety afloat, since numerous lake fishing situations involve the use of a boat. To begin with, if you are inexperienced at boat handling, you should complete a course aimed at acquainting you with safe boating procedures. The Coast Guard Auxiliary offers good courses in many areas of the country.

Let's review here the Coast Guard's suggestions for boating safety and apply them, where appropriate, to fly fishing on lakes.

1. Gasoline vapors are explosive. Being heavier than air, they settle in the lower parts of a boat. Although enclosed boats are seldom satisfactory fly fishing platforms, if you do plan to use such a craft, remember to close all doors, hatches and ports during fueling. Galley fires and pilot lights should be extinguished and smoking strictly prohibited during a fueling operation. The filling nozzle should be kept in contact with the fill pipe to prevent static spark. Avoid spilling fuel. Whenever possible, portable gas tanks should be

fueled out of the boat. Never use gasoline stoves, heaters or lights on board.

2. After fueling, thoroughly ventilate all compartments and check the machinery and fuel tank areas for fumes before starting the motor. The electrical ignition and starting system could ignite accumulated explosive vapors. Keep the fuel lines tight, the bilges clean. Make sure the tanks on large craft with immovable gas tanks are vented outboard and that fill pipes are located outboard of the coaming and extend to near the bottom of the tank. The fuel line should have an adequate filter.

3. Never overload your boat. Maintain adequate freeboard at all times to prevent swamping in heavy water. The water conditions, duration of the trip, predicted weather and experience of the boat operator all bear strongly on when you pull away from the dock, how far you should venture from shore and what types of water conditions you should attempt to tackle.

I'll never forget the time I went fishing with an ex officio guide who almost got me drowned. We'd traveled about ten miles when a stiff breeze came up that caused three- to five-foot high cresting rollers to churn down the lake in the direction from which we'd come. We were fishing out of an 18-foot wooden freighter canoe, a marvelous craft for navigating rough water. The boat was powered with a medium-sized outboard motor, 10 or 15 h.p. as I recall.

The water finally got so rough it became impossible to fish, so I suggested we head back to shore, whereupon my "guide" began to run cross-ways to the crashing waves. Several of the waves came close to swamping us. Finally, I became so concerned about my companion's boat handling ability I suggested we either go ashore and wait out the storm or head back to the dock along the lee shore. He took my suggestion quite testily, saying: "If you think you can do any better, you take over!" I knew he would resent it, but frankly didn't care. The guy had me scared half out of my wits by his ineptness. I took over and was able to bring the wonderful handling canoe back to the boat dock at the far end of the lake without incident. I'd been handling all sorts of boats in heavy water since childhood. I simply maneuvered the big freighter onto the back of a big roller and rode it and others most of the way back to camp without taking in more than a cup full of water.

Back on shore we were met by the fellow's wife who took one

look at him and exclaimed: "Why, where are your glasses? You know you can't see anything without your glasses!" Experiences like that one keep me from becoming embarrassed when I request the "wheel" from someone obviously lacking experience in rough-water boat handling.

4. Keep a sharp, alert lookout. This is terribly important when you're boating on lakes where there are submerged reefs, rock ledges extending out from the shoreline, numerous islands and other boats in the vicinity.

5. Be doubly careful when operating a boat near swimmers. Swimmers are often quite difficult to see in the water, especially if there's a chop or riffle.

6. Watch out that your wake doesn't capsize other craft in the area. Wake from a large boat can damage boats moored to docks and other shoreline property. You should travel through anchorages at slow speeds.

7. The firefighting and lifesaving equipment aboard your craft should be kept in perfect working order at all times and readily available.

8. Obey the Rules of the Road for boaters. Neglect of this is the greatest single cause of collisions, the Coast Guard says.

9. *Always* have children and nonswimmers wear lifesaving devices. Everyone aboard the boat should don a life jacket if circumstances suggest the slightest doubt of safety. If you encounter any resistance from your passengers about donning life jackets in a dubious safety situation, quickly explain that the conditions compel you to insist on life jackets for all hands. Don't back down, either. The boat operator is responsible for the safety of all aboard.

10. Know the capacity of your fuel tank and the crusing radius it allows. If necessary, carry additional gasoline in proper containers, taking special care to prevent the accumulation of gasoline vapor in confined spaces.

11. Do not tackle water conditions your judgment and experience dictate as unsafe. However, if you ever capsize it is usually best to remain with the boat if it continues to float.

12. Keep a clean boat, even if it's just a ten-foot car-top pram. Cleanliness diminishes the probability of fire.

13. Know the meanings of buoys. Never moor to one—it's a federal offense!

14. What would you do under any one of the following emergency situations: man overboard, fog, fire, bad leak in the hull, motor breakdown, collision, sudden violent storm? You'd better know before you head out on any lake!

15. Have an adequate anchor and sufficient line aboard to assure holding in a blow. You'll need anchor line at least six times the depth of the water to hold.

16. Boat hooks are not required equipment but very helpful in mooring and for retrieving hats, pets, life preservers and people who have fallen overboard.

17. Know the various distress signals. A recognized distress signal used on small boats is to slowly and repeatedly raise and lower the arms outstretched to each side.

18. Storm signals are meant for your safety. Learn them and be guided accordingly.

19. Operate your boat at high speeds only when you are clear of all other boats, bathers and obstructions and there are two persons aboard to maintain proper lookout.

20. Falls are the greatest causes of injury both afloat and ashore. Eliminate hazardous items on which persons might trip from your decks. If the boat is large enough provide adequate grabrails and make certain your passengers wear suitable footgear.

21. Always have up-to-date charts of the waters you navigate aboard. A compass is another must.

22. Always instruct at least one other person on board on the rudiments of starting and handling your boat in case you are disabled or fall overboard.

23. Keep electrical equipment and wiring in good condition. No knife switches or other arcing devices should be mounted in fuel or engine compartments. Allow ample ventilation around batteries.

24. Before departing on a boating trip to the fishing grounds, advise a responsible friend or relative about where you intend to fish. Give him a good description of your boat and keep him advised of any sudden changes in plans. And be sure to advise the same person when you return safely to prevent undue worry or the spread of any false alarms concerning your safety.

25. Do not test fire extinguishers by squirting them. The extinguisher might not work when needed. Follow approved instructions for checking fire extinguishers.

26. If you see a boat or buoy flying a red flag with a white diagonal—watch out! Skin divers are operating in the area. Stay clear at least 25 yards and keep your eyes peeled for signs of swimmers.

27. Finally, leave the booze back on shore. Boating and alcoholic beverages do not mix. There'll be plenty of time when you come in from the lake to enjoy a few pleasant "snorts" around the fire. Strong tea, coffee or hot chocolate are all excellent "warmer uppers" afloat. If your fishing companions insist on boozing it up in the boat, return them to shore. They'd have little chance for survival in any serious emergency afloat. The only really good angling companions on lakes are those who demonstrate sound judgment, restraint and moderation in consumption of alcoholic beverages.

To the experienced angler who's spent much of his life on or around the water, all of these basic safety precautions should be second nature. But, if you're a beginning boatman or limited in boating experience you'll be doing yourself and your companions a favor by enrolling in a class on boat handling and safety. Safe boating, no less than safe driving, is something we each must learn. A boat in the hands of an untrained or irresponsible handler can be just as lethal a vehicle as an auto in incompetent hands. Respect the water, then you'll live long enough to fish in it.

A few brief comments are in order on the subject of guides. A guide's job is to convey you safely to and from the fishing grounds, suggest possible methods of fishing after locating the fish for you and see to your comfort throughout the day. His job is basically to find the·fish. It's your responsibility to catch them.

Once you understand this basic relationship between guide and angler you will discover some other realities of life about guides. The most important is that guides are people, human beings like yourself. Guides react to attitudes and words, good humor or the lack of it, just as you do.

A good fishing guide is priceless. You can nurture your relationship with a good guide into warm and honest friendship by treating him as you would your regular fishing chums. However, insult his pride in his ability to find fish, treat him condescendingly and as an inferior being, make petulant, unwarranted demands, or blame him for your inability to catch the fish he finds for you, and you'll deserve exactly what you get—a long boatride.

On the other side of the coin, however, all guides are not good guides. Some are willing, but lack experience at either boat handling or fishing or both. Others are downright lazy and couldn't care less whether or not you ever catch fish. If you encounter a guide whose competence you question, if his boat handling methods appear to be dangerous or if he seems more interested in locating a nice place for a shore lunch than finding fish, then order him to return to camp and promptly inform the camp operator you want a more competent guide. You're paying good money for guide service; paying for the guide's judgment, skill and willingness to enhance your fishing. You have a right to expect these attributes from anyone who accepts the responsibility of guiding you. If the guide also happens to be a heck of a good Joe as well, then all the better.

One final thing about guides. Do not offer your guide intoxicating drinks. The Indian guides in some areas are prohibited by law from imbibing, although most of the ones I've encountered seem well-supplied with some sort of homemade moonshine. Just remember that in Canada you can get your guide, the camp owner and yourself in serious trouble by violating the "no liquor" rule with the guides.

11

Selected Flies for Lake Fishing

The nymphs, wet flies, dry flies and streamers whose dressings are described in this chapter comprise a representative group of patterns selected from the most effective lake flies used throughout the United States and Canada. Flies popular in every major lake angling sector of North America are included.

Notes about the origins and uses of certain flies have been included when the information is of significant historical value or essential to their effective use. Every dressing included here has proved itself to be a consistent producer of game fish over a span of at least five years. The author believes that listing several hundred fly dressings would confuse rather than assist an angler totally unfamiliar with lake fishing. By observing first hand the underwater life and adult insects in and about the lakes you fish, you should be able to adapt numerous flies in this book to your specific fly fishing needs.

Nymphs and Wet Flies

Alexandria

HOOKS: sizes 14 through 2, regular or heavy wire.

TIP: scarlet floss.

TAIL: three or four peacock sword feather flues.

BODY: flat silver tinsel.

RIBBING: embossed or oval silver tinsel.

WING: six or eight peacock sword feather flues.

DATA: A famous fly effective both in North America and Europe. Useful in lakes containing water beetles and leeches. Fished wet.

Beaverpelt Nymph

HOOKS: sizes 8 through 2, 2X long.

BODY: dark, brownish gray beaver under-fur, dubbed thickly.

HACKLE: Sparse. Dressed out of either soft, black hen neck hackle, or, more frequently, from a greenish gray Chinese pheasant rump feather.

DATA: Originated by Washington State Dept. of Game fisheries biologist, Don E. Earnest of Spokane, Wash. Earnest designed fly to suggest large, brownish dragonfly nymphs. Usually fished with a stripping retrieve on a sinking line. An extremely effective nymph!

Black Hackle, peacock body

HOOKS: size 14 through 2.

TAIL: a small bunch of black hackle fibres, though sometimes dressed with a scarlet tail.

BODY: green peacock herl, dressed thick and full, counterwound with black tying silk to provide strength and durability.

HACKLE: two or three turns of webby, black neck hackle.

DATA: Highly effective in most areas for trout, bass and panfish.

Black Midge Nymph

HOOKS: sizes 20 through 16, 1X short.

TAIL: a few wisps of black hackle.

BODY: moose mane quill; sometimes tied with dark brown thread.

FEELERS: a few black hackle wisps on each side of the head, tied short, but not clipped.

DATA: Originated by Dan Bailey, Livingston, Mont., and Gary Howells, Richmond, Calif., circa 1958. Imitates the pupa of the midge known as the "snow fly."

Black O'Lindsay

HOOKS: sizes 10 through 4, usually 2X long.

TAIL: brown over blue hackle fibres.

BODY: yellow yarn.

RIBBING: oval gold tinsel.

HACKLE: tied down as a throat, mixed brown and blue hackle fibres.

WING: underwing: a few peacock sword feather flues. Overwing: matched sections of barred gray mallard flank feather, although sometimes dressed in "rolled, downwing" wet fly style.

DATA: A popular and effective lake exploratory fly originating in British Columbia.

Blood Sucker

HOOKS: size 8 through 2, 4X long.

TAIL: a tuft of scarlet yarn or hackle fibres.

BODY: large diameter black chenille.

HACKLE: palmered, brown saddle hackle, clipped short. It's best to trim the hackle before tying it into the fly.

DATA: One of the best of the wooly worm type wet flies. Especially effective where there are dark leeches in the water.

Cahill, dark

HOOKS: size 12 and 10.
BODY: dubbed muskrat fur.
RIBBING: fine, flat, gold tinsel.
HACKLE: brown, tied as a beard.
WING: lemon wood duck, tied "rolled, downwing" style.
DATA: A reasonably good imitation of a drowned March Brown dun. Popular on eastern trout streams, this fly is best fished in lakes near the rocky shoreline areas where March Browns hatch.

Campbell's Fancy

HOOKS: sizes 18 through 6.
TAIL: golden pheasant crest feather.
BODY: flat gold tinsel.
HACKLE: furnace, tied as a beard.
WING: barred teal flank feather, "rolled downwing" style.
DATA: An effective wet fly, coast to coast.

Carey Special

HOOKS: sizes 12 through 2. Most often dressed in sizes 8 and 6.
TAIL: ground hog hairs, bear hairs, scarlet hackle wisps, pheasant rump feather wisps, or none.
BODY: tied variously out of virtually every conceivable shade of wool yarn, chenille, spun fur and hair. Brown, black, gray, green, olive, magenta and yellow are the most popular colors.

RIBBING: gold or silver tinsel, black silk rope, or none.

HACKLE: Three brownish or greenish brown Chinese pheasant rump feathers wound on as a dense, collar like hackle.

DATA: One of the "bread and butter" flies for deep-line fishing in the Pacific Northwest states and British Columbia. Designed by Dr. Lloyd A. Day, Quesnel, B.C., and first dressed by a Col. Carey circa 1925. This highly effective nymph represents a caddis fly pupa rising to the surface to hatch into an adult "sedge." The pattern was originally named the "Monkey-faced Louise," then later renamed and popularized by the late Joe Spurrier, a Kelowna, B. C., sporting goods dealer. By far the most important element of the dressing is the thickly tied rump feather hackle. Effective trolled, mooched or cast and retrieved.

Coachman, bucktail wing

HOOKS: sizes 14 through 2.
TAIL: scarlet hackle fibres.
BODY: green peacock herl, tied full.
HACKLE: dark brown, tied on as either a collar or a beard.
WING: white bucktail or impala, fairly sparse.
DATA: The Bucktail Coachman is one of the more universally effective flies throughout North America. If I had to select one pattern with which to do all of my lake fishing for all species of game fish, this would be it!

Cowdung

HOOKS: sizes 14 through 8.
BODY: dark olive floss or chenille.
HACKLE: brown, tied as a beard.
WING: matched sections of dark gray duck wing quill, or dark deer body hair.

Doc Spratley

HOOKS: sizes 10 through 4, with 8s and 6s most popular.
TAIL: grizzly hackle wisps.
BODY: black yarn.
RIB: silver tinsel; some tiers use flat, Scotch-embossed tinsel; others oval; still others prefer the plain, flat tinsel. It doesn't seem to make much difference.
HACKLE: grizzly, tied either as a sparse collar or beard.
WING: reddish brown fibres from the largest tail feathers of a cock, Chinese pheasant, dressed in "rolled, downwing" style.
HEAD: peacock herl.
DATA: Originated by the late "Dick" Prankard, a Mt. Vernon, Wash., sports shop operator circa 1949. Although the fly was originally designed as an "attractor" pattern for B. C. lake fishing, it bears a remarkable resemblence to a caddis pupa rising to hatch. The body is sometimes dressed out of dark olive colored wool. Extremely effective lake fly anywhere there are caddis flies.

Duck Lake Wooly Worm

HOOKS: sizes 8 through 2, 4X long.
BODY: medium or large-sized dark olive chenille.
HACKLE: grizzly, palmered.
DATA: Created by an unknown angler for use in famed Duck Lake, Mont., but effective virtually everywhere.

Ed Burke Nymph

HOOKS: sizes 14 through 10, regular shank.
TAIL: black hackle wisps.
TIP: gold tinsel.
BODY: black wool yarn, tied thickest near head.
RIBBING: fine, flat, gold tinsel on rear two-thirds of body.
HACKLE: black.
DATA: A famed eastern U.S. pattern useful throughout the country.

The Egg and I

HOOK: size 6.
BODY: rear two-thirds, flat silver tinsel; forward one-third, fluorescent red orange yarn, tied plump.
WING: two brown, drake mallard "nashua" flank feathers, tied flat, curving over the back.
DATA: This fly originated in Canada and was tied to suggest the alevin of the sockeye salmon. *The Egg and I* is used primarily in lakes where Kamloops rainbow trout feed on the immature salmon.

Fledermaus

HOOKS: sizes 10 through 1/0, 2X long.
BODY: muskrat fur, thickly dubbed; guard hairs are not removed from the fur.
WING: gray squirrel tail, tied slightly shorter than the body.
DATA: Originated by Jack Schneider of San Francisco, Calif., circa 1946. Widely used in larger sizes in Montana to simulate

large nymphs, small mice or bats that have fallen into the water. Very effective.

Green Drake Nymph

HOOKS: sizes 10 and 8, 2X long.
TAILS: two, small, honey dun neck hackle tips.
BODY: white fur, dubbed and picked out in the thorax area.
WING CASES: two, small jungle cock eye feathers.
HACKLE: pale honey dun.
DATA: Originated by C. M. Wetzel.

Guaranteed

HOOKS: sizes 10 through 6, 3X long.
TAIL: greenish brown cock Chinese pheasant rump feather wisps.
TIP: orange, hard-shell nymph floss.
BODY: green peacock herl.
HACKLE: metallic, blue green peacock breast feather, wrapped on as a sparse collar.
DATA: Originated by Karl G. Paulson, a veteran Pacific Northwest angler, circa 1961. This is a deadly fly on brook trout, cutthroat and rainbows. It's normally fished deeply, on a sinking line.

Heather Nymph

HOOKS: sizes 12 and 10, 2X or 3X long.
TAIL: scarlet hackle wisps.
BODY: rear half, insect green spun rabbit fur, ribbed with fine, oval gold tinsel; forward half, green peacock herl.
HACKLE: a sparse collar of webby, grizzly hackle.

DATA: Originated by newspaper outdoor writer, Fenton Roskelley, of Spokane, Wash., in 1960 to suggest general form and color of various damselfly and mayfly nymphs. This is unquestionably one of the most effective nymph flies ever designed and is fished both deep and near the surface. The fly was named in honor of Roskelley's daughter, Heather.

Gray Hackle, peacock body

HOOKS: sizes 16 through 2.
TAIL: scarlet hackle wisps, or none.
BODY: green peacock herl, tied full and counterwound with black tying silk for durability.
HACKLE: two or three turns of webby, grizzly neck hackle.
DATA: Fish either deep or shallow virtually anywhere in the United States and Canada. A consistently killing pattern.

Ginger Quill

HOOK: sizes 14 through 10.
TAIL: ginger hackle wisps.
BODY: peacock eye quill, stripped of all flues.
HACKLE: ginger, tied as a sparse beard.
WING: matched sections of gray duck wing quill, or barred, lemon wood duck dressed "rolled downwing" style.
DATA: The Ginger Quill is one of the basic mayfly patterns you'll need in both wet and dry versions.

Grizzly King

HOOKS: sizes 14 through 4.
TAIL: scarlet hackle wisps.

BODY: green yarn or floss.
RIBBING: flat or oval gold tinsel.
HACKLE: grizzly, dressed as a beard.
WING: barred, gray mallard flank feather, tied in "rolled, down-wing" style.
DATA: A popular, old-time favorite.

Hendrickson Nymph

HOOK: size 10, regular shank.
TAIL: wisps of barred mandarin (wood duck) flank feather.
BODY: a dubbed mixture of claret seal, beaver and gray for belly fur. Overall cast an unusual gray brown.
RIBBING: fine gold wire.
HACKLE: brownish partridge, bearded.
WING CASE: formed from a section of blue heron wing feather.

Henry's Lake Nymph (Yellow Goose)

HOOKS: sizes 8 and 6, regular shank.
TAIL: a bunch of gray squirrel tail hairs about the size of a small matchstick.
BODY: yellow, hot orange, red, insect green, brown, olive or black chenille; tied fat.
OVERBODY: a matchstick-sized bunch of gray squirrel tail hairs, tied in at butt of fly before wrapping chenille body, then pulled over the body, tied down at head and divided to form two sets of "whiskers."
DATA: This deadly nymph was originated for use at famed Henry's Lake, Idaho. Supposedly, it resembles a freshwater shrimp when retrieved rapidly and errat-ically through the water on a sinking fly line. The yellow and hot orange versions are generally the most effective.

Jock Scott

HOOKS: sizes 12 through 4.
TAIL: scarlet hackle wisps.
BODY: rear half, yellow floss; forward half, black floss.
RIBBING: fine flat gold tinsel.
HACKLE: guinea hen breast feather, bearded or tied as a collar.
WING: matched brown turkey wing feather splits; "married" scarlet and yellow strips on each side of wing.
DATA: Over a half-dozen variations of the Jock Scott are presently in use throughout the United States and Canada. I've yet to meet the fly dresser or angler willing to guess what this fly was designed to represent. Whatever it is, the Jock Scott is deadly, especially on lakes containing brook trout and Kamloops rainbows.

Kemp Bug

HOOKS: size 12 through 8, regular shank.
TAILS: three short tips of peacock herls.
BODY: peacock herl, tied fullest towards thorax.
HACKLE: furnace, tied as a sparse beard.
WING CASES: two short grizzly hackle tips tied in flat and slightly on top of body.
DATA: This fine nymph works especially well when mayfly nymphs are most active before hatches.

Montreal, dark

HOOKS: sizes 12 through 2.
TAIL: scarlet hackle wisps.
BODY: claret yarn or floss.
RIBBING: flat, gold tinsel.
HACKLE: claret, bearded.
WINGS: matched, mottled brown turkey wing feather sections.
DATA: Simply another of the "fancy" wet flies that entice fish, although no one seems to know why.

Nation's Silvertip Sedge

HOOKS: sizes 10 through 4, 1X long.
TAIL: small bunch of golden pheasant tippets.
BODY: two turns of medium flat silver tinsel, the remainder dubbed green fur or yarn.
RIBBING: fine oval gold tinsel.
WINGS: matched light mottled turkey wing feather sections.
HACKLE: badger, tied as a collar ahead of the wings.
DATA: Originated by British Columbian Bill Nation, for fishing on Kamloops trout lakes. Suggests a green bodied caddis fly pupa.

Needle Fly Nymph

HOOKS: sizes 10 and 8, long shanked.
BODY: flat, silver tinsel; dress thin, untapered.
HACKLE: a single, brown Chinese rooster rump feather tied as a collar.
HEAD: peacock herl.
DATA: Originated by Dawn Holbrook of Seattle, Wash., in 1933 to suggest damselfly nymphs. Other verisons are dressed with herl, black, red, yellow, or green wool bodies.

Nylon Nymph

HOOKS: sizes 14 through 6.
TAIL: a few wisps from a barred, gray mallard flank feather.
BODY: white floss, overlaid with clear, nylon leader material.
WING CASES: small jungle cock eye feathers (2) tied slightly divided on top.
HEAD: white.
DATA: Created by Ken McLeod (father of noted steelhead fisherman, George McLeod) in 1941 to suggest newly matched perch fry and various translucent nymphs. Author sometimes applies a pink floss underbody, instead of white, with excellent results.

Parmachene Belle

HOOKS: sizes 14 through 2.
TAIL: mixed scarlet and white hackle wisps.
BODY: yellow floss or mohair.
RIBBING: flat gold tinsel.
HACKLE: mixed scarlet and white.
WINGS: matched sections ot white duck wing feathers or white polar bear or bucktail; narrow scarlet feather strips at sides of wings.
DATA: Another "oldie" that's frequently useful for brookies, cutthroats, bass, crappies and bluegills.

Professor

HOOKS: sizes 14 through 2.
TAIL: scarlet hackle wisps.
BODY: yellow floss or mohair.
RIBBING: gold tinsel.
HACKLE: brown, bearded.
WING: barred, gray mallard flank feather, dressed in "rolled, downwing" style.
DATA: Useful throughout the Unit-

ed States and Canada for trout, bass and panfish.

Royal Coachman

HOOK: sizes 16 through 2, regular or long shank.

TAIL: scarlet hackle wisps, or golden pheasant tippets.

TIP: (optional), gold tinsel.

BODY: peacock herl butt and thoracic joints with scarlet floss or yarn between them.

HACKLE: natural, red brown gamecock, bearded or tied as a collar ahead of the wing.

WING: white bucktail, or matched sections from white duck or goose wing feathers.

CHEEKS: (optional), jungle cock eye feathers.

DATA: The Royal Coachman would have to rank either number one or number two in the top ten list of most effective lake flies for virtually all freshwater gamefish species.

Sand Fly Nymph

HOOKS: sizes 14 through 8.

TAIL: short tuft of white marabou feathers.

BODY: brown floss, tapered.

RIBBING: yellow thread or floss.

HACKLE: ginger, tied as a sparse collar.

DATA: Originated by Mr. Herbert Butler circa 1943 to simulate a small water beetle that has trapped an air bubble. A wonderful nymph for rainbow trout.

T. D. C. Nymph

HOOK: size 10, 1X long, 1X fine.

BODY: small-sized black chenille, tapered larger towards head.

RIBBING: four or five turns of narrow, oval silver tinsel.

HEAD: three or four turns of fluffy, white ostrich herl.

DATA: Originated by Richard B. Thompson, a fisheries biologist with the U. S. Fish and Wildlife Service, to suggest midge pupae. In order to be effective this fly requires a dead slow retrieve. Most useful in near-surface fishing with a floating or sink-tip line.

Teal and Red

HOOKS: sizes 12 through 6.

TAIL: small bunch of golden pheasant tippets.

TIP: gold tinsel.

BODY: dark red dubbed fur, or scarlet yarn.

HACKLE: olive, bearded.

WING: a barred, teal flank feather, dressed in "rolled, downwing" style.

DATA: Teal and Red is one of the most useful of the "oldies" on trout lakes.

Thunderbug

HOOKS: sizes 8 through 2, 2X or 3X long.

TAIL: a few black bear hairs, tied short.

BODY: dubbed muskrat, beaver or fox fur, dressed very full and tapered larger towards the head. The guard hairs are dubbed in and later picked out with a needle near the head.

RIBBING: fine, gold or silver wire.

DATA: One of the most effective of all the fur-bodied nymphs suggesting the underwater forms of dragonflies and damselflies.

Trueblood's Otter Nymph

HOOKS: sizes 10 and 8, 1X short.

TAIL: a few wisps of partridge hackle.

BODY: otter fur, mixed with a small amount of either natural seal or olive-dyed seal and dubbed in.

HACKLE: partridge hackle, bearded.

HEAD: Ted ties the head with green thread to indicate a "weighted" nymph, tan thread on unweighted versions.

DATA: Originated circa 1950 by outdoor writer, Ted Trueblood, of Nampa, Idaho, to simulate scuds and various insect nymphs. The fly is usually fished on a fast-sinking line near the lake bottom, or on a surface line with a retrieve that causes it to rise towards the surface.

White Miller

HOOKS: sizes 14 through 2/0.

TAIL: scarlet hackle wisps.

BODY: white chenille.

HACKLE: white.

WINGS: matched sections from white duck or goose wing quills, or white bucktail.

DATA: Effective on trout, bass and panfish.

Yellow Spider

HOOKS: sizes 10 through 2.

TAIL: scarlet hackle wisps.

BODY: yellow yarn or mohair.

RIBBING: gold tinsel.

HACKLE: dyed-yellow, barred mallard flank feather tied on as a collar.

DATA: An adaptation of the old, Scottish, "Lough Earn," useful on trout, bass and panfish. An effective variation is dressed with a green body.

Dry Flies

Adams

HOOKS: sizes 18 through 8, fine wire.

TAIL: mixed, brown and grizzly hackle wisps.

BODY: dubbed gray muskrat fur.

HACKLE: mixed, brown and grizzly.

WINGS: grizzly hackle tips, dressed upright and divided or "spent."

DATA: One of the most generally useful dry flies on North American waters.

Black Drake

HOOKS: sizes 14 and 12, fine wire.

TAIL: a few wisps of natural black gamecock hackle.

BODY: stripped peacock eye quill.

WING: a half-dozen gray deer body hairs tied in behind the hackle.

HACKLE: natural black, very sparse.

DATA: Deadly when Black Drakes are hatching! This version which originated in Oregon is a superb floater. It resembles another popular inland northwest fly called the "Black Hannah," which is dressed similarly, except that it has a tail of black impala hairs and *dyed* black hackle.

Blue Dun

HOOKS: sizes 14 through 10, fine wire.

TAIL: pale, blue dun hackle wisps.

BODY: gray fur, dubbed.

HACKLE: blue dun gamecock, dyed or natural.

WINGS: matched sections of gray duck wing quills, tied upright and divided, or a half-dozen gray deer body hairs. If a hairwing is used, tie in behind the hackle.

DATA: Another of the "basic" lake flies no angler should be without.

Brown Ant

HOOKS: sizes 16 and 14, extra-fine wire.

TAIL: a few brown, calf tail hairs, tied short.

BODY: brown floss or thread.

WINGS: tiny section of gray mallard primary feather tied flat over the body and trimmed round on the end.

HACKLE: two or three turns of a very stiff natural red brown gamecock hackle, with a "V" clipped out underneath.

DATA: Originated by the late Milo C. "Cap" Godfrey. This killing lake fly simulates a brownish gray midge that's just hatched.

Flying Ant

HOOKS: sizes 10 and 8, fine wire.

BODY: formed with black silk floss over a thread base to the shape of an ant's body, then heavily lacquered.

WINGS: two, blue dun hackle tips tied flat and divided like an ant's. Sometimes brownish tinged grizzly hackle tips are substituted.

HACKLE: black gamecock, with a "V" clipped out underneath so the fly rides quite low in the water.

DATA: Usually effective whenever fish feed on winged ants.

Green Drake Spinner (Coffin Fly)

HOOKS: sizes 10 and 8, with 8 most popular.

TAIL: a few wisps from a cock Chinese pheasant tail feather.

BODY: dubbed cream colored fur.

WING: a barred teal breast feather, dressed rolled and divided, upright; or black hackle tips.

HACKLE: dark badger gamecock.

Green Sedge

HOOKS: sizes 10 through 6.

BODY: green wool yarn, sheathed with barred mallard flank feather.

RIBBING: green floss or thread.

WINGS: sandy colored Chinese pheasant body feathers or barred, gray mallard breast feathers tied flat over body behind hackle, conclave sides down.

HACKLE: grizzly.

DATA: Originated for use on Kamloops trout lakes in British Columbia, but useful wherever large, green bodied caddis flies abound. Often fished by retrieving along surface to simulate the scurrying of the caddis flies.

Grizzly Wulff

HOOKS: sizes 14 through 8, light wire.

TAIL: a fairly thick bunch of brown, white-tailed deer body hairs.

BODY: pale, yellow silk floss; sometimes lacquered to form a hard body.

WINGS: brown, white-tailed deer hair from near the base of the animal's tail, dressed upright and divided into two uniform bunches.

HACKLE: mixed brown and grizzly gamecock.

DATA: Created by famed fly dresser Dan Bailey of Livingston, Mont., in 1936 to simulate certain mayflies and stone flies fluttering their wings before leaving the water. Deadly on trout, bass, panfish and arctic grayling.

Hendrickson, dark

HOOKS: sizes 14 and 12.

TAIL: a few wisps from a lemon

wood duck flank feather.

BODY: dubbed dark gray fur.

WINGS: lemon wood duck feather, dressed upright, rolled and divided.

HACKLE: dark blue dun gamecock.

DATA: Suggests a male, Blue Quill dun. Good for trout and grayling, wherever "blue duns" are found.

Horner Deer Hair (Goofus Bug)

HOOKS: sizes 12 through 8.

TAIL: a matchstick-sized bunch of brownish gray deer body hairs.

BODY: a matchstick-sized bunch of brownish gray deer body hair, tied in at tail by butts then pulled forward over top of hook to form a bulbous-shaped body. The ends of the hair are tied upright and divided to form the wings.

HACKLE: mixed brown and grizzly gamecock.

WINGS: (see instructions for tying body.)

DATA: Originated by Jack Horner of San Francisco, Calif. Extremely useful on both lakes and streams. One of the better variations is tied with yellow thread and with a yellow floss underbody.

Joe's Hopper

HOOKS: sizes 12 through 6, 2X or 3X long.

TAIL: scarlet hackle wisps, or a tuft of scarlet yarn.

BODY: yellow wool yarn, first formed into a short loop protruding slightly past the bend of the hook, then wrapped forward in the usual way; palmered with clipped brown hackle.

WINGS: matched sections from brown turkey wing feathers, lacquered, trimmed to approximate shape of grasshopper wings and tied along upper sides of the body.

HACKLE: mixed brown and grizzly gamecock.

DATA: This fly is not only one of the most popular, but also one of the more effective of the numerous flies dressed to simulate grasshoppers. Many tiers vary the colors to match those of grasshoppers in their particular regions.

Light Caddis

HOOKS: sizes 10 and 8, 1X fine.

TAIL: ginger hackle wisps, tied thick and short.

BODY: ginger nylon yarn, dressed thickly and palmered with ginger saddle hackle.

WING: ginger bucktail, relatively short.

HACKLE: ginger gamecock or saddle, tied in front of the wing.

HEAD: ginger colored thread.

DATA: Originated by E. H. "Polly" Rosborough of Chiloquin, Ore. The fly should have a pronounced dark ginger cast overall. Delete the tail for a wet version.

Light Cahill

HOOKS: sizes 12 and 10, fine wire.

TAIL: a few wisps of barred wood duck breast or flank feather.

BODY: dubbed cream colored fur from the belly of a red fox.

WINGS: barred wood duck feather, dressed upright, rolled and divided.

HACKLE: light ginger gamecock.

DATA: This is a very effective lake pattern in both the East and the West, especially useful on cutthroat and rainbow trout waters.

March Brown (F. F. F. Mayfly)

HOOK: size 12, fine wire.

TAIL: mixed natural black and brown hackle wisps.

BODY: dark brown wool yarn or dubbed fur.

RIBBING: beige thread.

WINGS: grizzly hackle tips, dressed upright and divided, or white for more visibility.

HACKLE: mixed natural black and red brown gamecock.

DATA: Created by outdoor writer Fenton Roskelley, about 1966 to simulate dark brown mayflies. This fly was named in honor of the Federation of Fly Fishermen. It is an excellent early season lake pattern, the most effective of all the March Brown patterns tried by the author to date.

Mosquito

HOOKS: sizes 16 through 10, fine wire.

TAIL: grizzly hackle wisps.

BODY: stripped peacock eye quill, or black floss ribbed with white thread.

WINGS: small grizzly hackle tips, dressed flat and divided over the back.

HACKLE: grizzly, dressed sparse ahead of the wings.

DATA: This is an extremely useful early season fly virtually everywhere. It is on the must list for trout and grayling.

Red Quill

HOOKS: size 12, fine wire.

TAIL: natural red brown gamecock.

BODY: stripped peacock eye quill, dyed red.

WINGS: matched sections of gray duck wing feather.

HACKLE: natural red brown gamecock.

Renegade

HOOKS: sizes 16 through 8, fine wire.

TIP: fine, flat, gold tinsel.

AFT HACKLE: natural red brown gamecock.

BODY: peacock herl.

FORE HACKLE: white or natural cream gamecock.

DATA: Without question the Renegade is one of the most popular and effective dressings available to the angler seeking surface action from cutthroat trout, sometimes eliciting "action" in the absence of insect hatches.

Salmon Candy

The Salmon Candy is actually four distinct flies representing a specific caddis fly's hatching efforts. Stages one and two represent the pupa, just prior to the actual hatching out of the adult insect. Stages three and four suggest hatched adult insects.

Stage 1

HOOK: size 8.

TAIL: a few deer body hairs, dressed short and sparsely.

BODY: medium-dark olive wool.

THORAX: take one turn of brown hackle, then form a "collar" similar to that of a muddler minnow from a small bunch of deer body hair, very sparse. Trim away most of the hackle and the deer hair, leaving only a few strands.

DATA: All four versions of the Salmon Candy were created by Lloyd Frese, a C.P.A. in Bend,

Ore. They represent a sedge that hatches at famed Hosmer Lake, Ore. This version is used when the surface of the lake is calm.

Stage 2

HOOK: size 8.
TAIL: same as in Stage 1.
OVERBODY: deer body hairs tied in at tail, then pulled as a bunch over the underbody and tied off at head, leaving a small, clipped head.
UNDERBODY: same as in Stage 1.
HACKLE: brown, palmered sparsely.
DATA: Use when there's a riffle on the water.

Stage 3

HOOK: size 8.
TAIL: none.
BODY: same as in first two stages.
OVERBODY: gray deer body hair.
HACKLE: natural red and grizzly mixed.
WING: gray deer body hair over back as long as hook bend; butts tied forward to form short thorax; butt ends clipped to form a small head.
DATA: This version is considered the most effective of the top-water versions.

Stage 4

HOOK: size 8.
TAIL: none.
BODY: same as first three stages.
HACKLE: gray deer body hair, tied at roughly 45-degree angle over back of fly.
WING: mixed brown and grizzly, dressed sparsely.
DATA: Seems to be most effective near the conclusion of a hatch.

Sand Fly Bucktail

HOOKS: sizes 10 and 8, 2X fine, 2X long.

TAIL: natural brown bucktail, same length as body, or slightly longer.
BODY: yellow wool yarn, a pale shade preferred.
RIBBING: dark brown floss or thread
WING: natural brown deer body hair, tied behind hackle in semi-upright position.
HACKLE: natural red gamecock (brown), tied bushy.
DATA: Originated circa 1947 by the late Milo C. "Cap" Godfrey to simulate the large Yellow Drake mayflies that hatch on lakes. Very effective.

Tom Thumb

HOOKS: sizes 8 and 6.
TAIL: a buch of natural gray or brown deer body hairs, match-stick-size, dressed quite short.
BODY: Take a substantial bunch of natural deer body hairs (the size of two or three matchsticks), tie it in by the butts, then pull forward and tie in at the head. Pull ends upright to form a single, somewhat spread wing. Support the wing with a thread base wrapping.
HACKLE: grizzly (optional).
DATA: This somewhat unusual looking concoction was originated in Canada to simulate the newly hatched adult caddis fly as it extends its wings upward and forward momentarily after emerging from the pupa. Tie lots of these flies if you plan to use them at all. They are fragile and the fishes' teeth shred them in no time. Each fly is good for about five fish, at the most.

Western Bee

HOOKS: sizes 12 through 6, fine wire.

BODY: four alternate bands of black and orange chenille or wool yarn. Yarn floats longer than chenille. One enthusiast I know dyes kapok the desired shades and spins it on thread like fur dubbin. Not a bad idea!

HACKLE: natural red gamecock, dressed bushy.

WINGS: natural gray brown deer body hair, dressed either in front of, or behind the hackle. I prefer the rear-wing version.

DATA: This old-time favorite can be counted to be effective under a wide range of late spring and early fall conditions.

Streamer Flies

Atom Bomb

HOOK: size 1/0, long shank.

TAIL: two yellow saddle hackle tips.

BODY: tubular silver mylar, picked out underneath to simulate shape of a minnow's body.

WINGS: underwing: yellow marabou. Overwing: white bucktail topped by a few strands of peacock herl.

HACKLE: brown saddle, bearded.

HEAD: black.

EYES: white, with red iris and black pupils.

DATA: One of a series of effective trolling flies for large brown trout brought to famed Portland, Ore., fly dresser Audrey Joy by George and Helen Van Oss. The gray version has a brown hackle tip tail, same body and gray marabou over white bucktail wing topped with brown bucktail. Hackle is brown and eyes are white with red pupils.

Black Leech

HOOKS: sizes 8 through 2, regular or long shank.

TAIL: none, or scarlet hackle wisps, or two black hackle tips tied splayed out.

BODY: peacock herl, dressed rather full.

RIBBING: oval silver tinsel (optional).

HACKLE: black, dressed as a collar (optional).

WINGS: two black saddle hackles, dressed splayed with concave sides facing out.

DATA: Fish this killing pattern of Canadian origin with a slow, undulating retrieve or troll. It's usually the most productive when used in conjunction with a sinking fly line.

Black Ghost

HOOKS: sizes 10 through 2, long shank.

TAIL: yellow hackle wisps.

BODY: black silk floss, dressed rather full, tapered at both ends, but larger towards front.

RIBBING: medium flat silver tinsel.

HACKLE: small bunch of yellow hackle fibres tied in as a beard.

WINGS: four white saddle hackles, concave sides inward.

CHEEKS: jungle cock eye feathers.

DATA: This great favorite since the 1920s is an outstanding producer when fished for landlocked salmon, brook trout, browns and rainbows throughout the U. S. and Canada. Effective retrieved or trolled.

Colonel Bates

HOOKS: sizes 10 through 2, long shank.

TAIL: a small section of scarlet duck wing feather. (Note: Author prefers scarlet hackle wisps.)

BODY: medium flat silver tinsel.

THROAT: a small bunch of dark brown hackle fibres.

WINGS: two yellow saddle hackles tied inside of two slightly longer white saddle hackles.

SHOULDERS: barred teal breast feathers, tied half as long as the wing.

CHEEKS: jungle cock eye feathers.

HEAD: red.

DATA: Originated by Mrs. Carrie G. Stevens of Madison, Me. It is especially effective in turbid lakes, and a must fly on a basic list for landlocked salmon and brook trout. The pattern is also highly effective on crappies and bass.

Edson Dark Tiger

HOOKS: sizes 10 through 2, 4X or 6X long shank.

TIP: fine flat gold tinsel.

TAIL: two small yellow hackle tips tied back-to-back with concave sides facing out.

BODY: small yellow chenille.

THROAT: tips of two small scarlet neck hackles.

WINGS: a small bunch of brown bucktail, dyed yellow, extending slightly beyond the bend of the hook.

CHEEKS: small jungle cock eye feathers.

HEAD: yellow.

DATA: Originated in 1929 by William R. Edson, Portland. Me. Useful on landlocked salmon, trout of most species, largemouth and smallmouth bass, and panfish. This fly is also a killer on northern pike, but the pike's sharp teeth rip the chenille body quickly to shreds.

Gray Ghost

HOOKS: sizes 10 through 2, long shank.

TIP: fine flat silver tinsel.

BODY: orange floss, thinly dressed.

THROAT: four strands of peacock herl under which is tied a small bunch of white bucktail, below which is tied a golden pheasant crest feather (curving upwards). The peacock is the same length as the wing, the bucktail a bit shorter and the crest feather as long as the shoulder.

WINGS: tie in a golden pheasant crest feather the same length you intend for the hackle wings. Over the crest feather tie in four olive gray saddle hackles, concave sides facing inwards.

SHOULDER: wide silver pheasant body feathers, one-third the length of the saddle hackle wing.

CHEEKS: jungle cock eye feathers.

DATA: Created by Mrs. Carrie G. Stevens to suggest smelt and other lake forage fishes. This pattern is extremely popular in the eastern U. S.

Muddler Minnow

HOOKS: sizes 10 through 1/0, 3X long shank.

TAIL: a pair of mottled brown turkey wing sections.

BODY: gold tinsel.

HACKLE: white-tail deer body hairs.

WINGS: brown impala over white impala, same length as hook bend; a pair of mottled brown turkey wing sections tied over the impala, same length.

HEAD: clipped white-tail deer gray body hair, shaped round and full.

DATA: Originated by Don Gapen, Nipigon, Ont., circa 1950 to represent the sculpin minnow. Primarily a stream fly, but it has been known to be very effective in lakes where game fish feed on the sculpin. The author has even caught steelheads (sea-run rainbow trout) on this pattern in Washington and Idaho rivers.

Nine-Three

HOOKS: sizes 10 through 2, long shank.
BODY: medium flat silver tinsel.
WINGS: first tie a small bunch of white bucktail to extend beyond the hook bend. Then, over the bucktail, tie in flat three medium green saddle hackles. Over these tie in upright a pair of natural black saddle or neck hackles in the normal fashion.
CHEEKS: jungle cock eye feathers.
DATA: Effective on trout, landlocked salmon, bass and panfish. The trolling version for salmon is usually dressed on tandem hooks joined by nylon.

Northern Pike Streamers

HOOKS: sizes 2 through 3/0. I prefer the Mustad No. 3407Z, a very stout commercial saltwater hook because of its ability to stay sharp once filed to a needle-sharp, triangular-shaped point. The pike's hard mouth parts tend to dull some of the conventional freshwater streamer hooks.
BODY: flat silver, or tubular silver mylar, or silver "chenille" tinsel, heavily lacquered.
WINGS: four saddle hackles, tied in bicolored pairs, splayed with concave sides facing out. Red and white, and yellow and red have produced the best results for me. In the fall, when pike

are in deep weed beds near drop-offs, a fly dressed with all fluorescent red wings is sometimes very effective.
HACKLE: a thick collar of hackles matching the wings.
DATA: fish these flies very slowly.

Perch Fry

HOOKS: sizes 10 through 2, 6X long.
TAIL: a small bunch of green polar bear hairs.
BODY: insect-green spun fur dressed medium-full.
RIBBING: medium oval gold tinsel.
THROAT: a small tuft of scarlet hackle fibres (optional).
WING: green, over yellow, over white polar bear hair, dressed sparsely the same length as the tail.
CHEEKS: jungle cock eye feathers (optional).
HEAD: medium olive green.
DATA: Originated by the author in 1963 to attract crappies and large rainbow trout in perch infested impoundments and reservoirs. Very effective early in the spring in smaller sizes. Later in the season large sizes are preferred.

Supervisor

HOOKS: sizes 10 through 2, long shank.
TAIL: a short thin piece of red yarn.
BODY: medium flat silver tinsel.
RIBBING: narrow oval silver tinsel (optional).
WING: a small bunch of white bucktail, over which are tied four light blue saddle hackles.
TOPPING: six strands of peacock herl as long as the wing.
SHOULDERS: pale green hackles,

each two-thirds the wing length and the same width.

CHEEKS: jungle cock eye feathers.

DATA: Originally an idea of Joseph S. Stickney, Saco, Me. Suggests a smelt. Excellent fly on land-locked salmon, trout and bass. Author especially likes to use this fly in the upper midwestern region for largemouth bass.

Whitlock's Sculpin

HOOKS: sizes 10 through 1/0, 3X long, weighted.

THREAD: tan Nymo.

TAIL: none.

BODY: dubbed with cream colored fur.

RIBBING: medium oval gold tinsel.

WINGS: a small bunch of red or gray fox squirrel tail hairs, and a pair of varigated Cree neck hackles, tied to lie flat.

COLLAR: two broad banded breast feathers from a mallard hen, hen pheasant or a prairie chicken.

HACKLE: antelope hair and dark brown deer body hair.

HEAD: bands of clipped deer hair in brandy brown, gray and dark brown, shaped wide and flat.

DATA: This killing pattern by David Whitlock of Bartlesville, Okla., is usually dressed with 10 to 20 turns of lead wire weighting. It is very slow to construct, but well worth the effort. Famed Montana fly dresser, Dan Bailey, describes this fly as being a better imitation of the sculpin than the spuddler. Useful in virtually any lake or river containing sculpin minnows and large predatory trout. Fish near the bottom on a sinking line.

Yellow and White Bucktail

HOOKS: sizes 8 through 2, regular or long shank.

BODY: medium flat silver tinsel.

WING: a medium-size bunch of white bucktail, over which is tied a small bunch of yellow bucktail.

HEAD: yellow.

DATA: By far one of the most effective flies for crappies and large trout in lakes containing shiners or perch.

BIBLIOGRAPHY

Bates, Joseph D. Jr. *Streamer Fly Tying and Fishing,* rev. ed. The Stockpole Company. 1966.

Blades, William F. *Fishing Flies and Fly Tying,* Stackpole and Heck, Inc. 1951.

Gardner, A. E. *The Early Stages of Odonata,* Proc. Trans. S. London Ent. Nat. Hist. Soc. 1951.

Gerlach and Roskelley. "Flies of the Northwest," rev. ed. I.E.F.F.C., 1970.

Gerlach and Roskelley. "Rehabilitation—Boon or Boondoggle." Unpublished.

Gordon, Sid W. *How to Fish from Top to Bottom,* rev. ed. The Stockpole Company. 1957.

Imms, A. D. *A General Textbook of Entomology,* rev. ed. Methuen & Co., Ltd. 1957.

Koller, Larry. *A Treasury of Angling,* New York: A Ridge Press Book—Golden Press, 1963.

Morgan, Ann Haven. *Field Book of Ponds and Streams,* New York-London: G. Putnam's & Sons, 1930.

Munz, P. A. "A venational study of the sub-order Zygoptera," Mem. Am. Ent. Soc., 3: 1919.

Needham and Lloyd. *Life of Inland Water,* Charles C. Thomas Publisher. 1930.

Needham, N. T. "Prodrome for a manual of the Dragon Flies of North America," Trans. Am. Ent. Soc., 77. 1951.

Needham, Traver and Hsu. *The Biology of Mayflies,* Ithaca. 1935.

O.R.R.C. Study Report 7. "Sport Fishing Today and Tomorrow," U. S. Dept. of Int. 1962.

Rice, F. Philip. "America's Favorite Fishing," *Outdoor Life*—Harper & Row. 1964.

Swain, Ralph B. Ph.D. *The Insect Guide,* Doubleday & Company, Inc. and the American Garden Guild Inc. 1948.

Walden, Howard T. 2nd. *Familiar Freshwater Fishes of America,* Harper & Row. 1964.

Welch, Paul S. Ph.D. *Limnology,* McGraw-Hill Book Company, Inc. 1935.